Ready or Not

✓ *Inside You'll Find:*

The Future
How Do I Stand

Yes No

❑ ❑ I know approximately what my Social Security and pension income will be in retirement.

❑ ❑ I have a financial savings plan for retirement and am out of debt.

❑ ❑ I know the approximate future income from my investments—IRA and savings.

❑ ❑ I have completed a net worth statement.

❑ ❑ I have analyzed my cash flow—monthly and yearly.

❑ ❑ I have discussed finances with my spouse.

❑ ❑ I have an up-to-date will, a power of attorney and health care proxy.

❑ ❑ I have my important papers—including my will—where my family can find them.
I have reviewed the papers with my spouse.

❑ ❑ I practice good health habits, walk daily, don't smoke, and drink in moderation.

❑ ❑ I have a physical examination each year.

❑ ❑ I've checked my health insurance coverage, both now and for retirement.

❑ ❑ I've checked my home for safety and maintenance.

❑ ❑ I've discussed retirement plans—where to live, what to do with time—with my spouse
and family.

❑ ❑ I maintain relationships with friends and am involved in at least one social activity—
volunteer work, civic or religious activities, etc.

❑ ❑ I am enrolled in an education or skill-advancement course that interests me and will open
doors for new experiences in retirement.

❑ ❑ I am aware that many women are still in the workforce in their early 60s and am
prepared for a longer work life.

❑ ❑ I know that all will not go as planned and have built a financial safety net in my planning.
I will take into account losing a job, inflation, health care and a long life.

❑ ❑ I am planning my retirement, knowing that the life expectancy chart is the average
a person is expected to live. I may live longer. Many live close to 100.

2019
46th Edition

Ready or Not

Your Retirement Planning Guide

By
Elizabeth M. McFadden

Updates made by
Staff members of the
International Foundation of Employee Benefit Plans

Past Contributors

Jim Caulder
Social Security Specialist,
Informed Decisions

Artwork by
Bill Kresse

International Foundation *if*®
OF EMPLOYEE BENEFIT PLANS
Education | Research | Leadership

The Parable of the Rose

A certain man planted a rosebush and watered it faithfully. Before it bloomed, he examined it. He saw the bud that would soon blossom; but, noticing thorns upon the stem, he thought, "How can any beautiful flower come from a plant burdened with so many sharp thorns?" Saddened by this thought, he neglected to water the rosebush and, before it could bloom, it died.

So it is with many people. Within every soul there is a rose—the Godlike qualities planted in us at birth, growing amid the thorns of our faults. Many of us look at ourselves and see only the thorns, the defects. We despair, thinking that nothing good can possibly come from us. We neglect to water the good within us, and eventually it dies. We never realize our potential.

Some people do not see the rose within themselves; someone else must show it to them.

One of the greatest gifts a person can possess is the ability to reach past the thorns within others and find the rose. This is the characteristic of love—to look at a person, know their true faults, and accept that person into your life, recognizing the nobility in their soul and helping them to realize that they can overcome their faults.

If we show our loved ones the rose, they will conquer their thorns. Only then will they blossom many times over.

> "You cannot escape the responsibility of tomorrow by evading it today."
>
> —*Abraham Lincoln*
>
> "Twenty years from now, you will be more disappointed by the things you didn't do than by the ones you did do."
>
> —*Mark Twain*
>
> "A journey of a thousand miles must begin with a single step."
>
> —*Lao Tzu*

The Time of Your Life

Today more than ever before, aging is an opportunity, not a problem. Americans in general are living longer, healthier, more active lives. When you retire, you have the chance to pursue your happiness—without the responsibility or demands of work. And you have the energy and resources to achieve personal goals of travel, hobbies and education.

Have you prepared yourself and your family for this new opportunity? This book is designed to help you look clearly and positively at the changes and decisions of retirement. From financial planning, to health, to family matters, or to a new job, full- or part-time, we address clearly and directly the financial, physical and emotional concerns you may have about retirement.

An Aging Nation

The first thing to know about aging in America is that "everybody's doing it."

Between now and 2030, the aged will become a dominant segment of America's population.

People are living longer than ever before. In 1900, average life expectancy was 50 years. A 65-year-old today has a 50% chance of reaching age 93 and a 25% chance of reaching age 98, according to the National Center for Health Statistics. Increases in life spans are redefining retirement; rather than growing old in retirement, the focus is now on living *young* in retirement. The increased life span comes with the concern of outliving your money.

Better health care, nutrition awareness, a higher standard of living, earlier retirement—all have contributed to longer, more vibrant lives, affirming Elizabeth Browning's lines, "Come, grow old with me, the best is yet to come."

You may be reading this book and saying, "I will not be retiring for a long time." Think again. More and more of us are facing a choice sooner than anticipated.

Much of the information covered in *Ready or Not* is relevant at all ages and stages at work… and, as the title suggests, is intended to make you aware of the need to start planning for your future *today*.

Ready or Not

Ready or Not is designed to help you make your future years satisfying, enriching and comfortable. Each chapter deals with issues of importance. Experts and professionals have contributed specific, detailed information in clear, concise

TALK IT OVER…

1

Aging

Did You Know That

- More than 40.3 million people age 65 years or older live in the United States, constituting 13% of the population.

- The ability to learn new skills and acquire new information remains relatively unchanged from age 20 through age 60. Intellectual powers do not decline as rapidly as people think. "You can't teach an old dog new tricks" is true only if the "old dog" happens to believe this proverb!

- We achieve peak mass muscle strength in our early 40s. By simply walking or gardening, you can help slow down the loss. Exercise has benefits at any age. Check with your doctor before starting any exercise activity.

- Comprehension and vocabulary ability holds strong through age 60. Physical dexterity and reaction to stimuli reach a peak at age 18, with a slow decline after age 40. The ability to learn, though, is relatively unaffected by age.

- Of all married couples over 65, the percentage living in their own households is 80%. For those individuals not married, 50% live on their own.

- The average couple has 35–40 years of partial leisure after their children are grown.

- 90% of persons over 65 report relative freedom from chronic health problems that could limit their activities. Two factors that are important to extended health and happiness are: (1) an understanding of one's self (physically, mentally, and socially) and (2) good medical care in early and later life.

- About 80% to 120% of preretirement income is necessary to enable the retired person to maintain his or her previous level of spending and living. Some expenses, including work-related expenses—eating out, clothes, transportation—and taxes, will decrease. Other expenses, such as health care, travel and leisure activities, energy expenses, and costs incurred helping parents or children, may increase. And inflation will affect buying power. The Employee Benefit Research Institute found that, in the first 5 years of retirement, more than 50% of retirees spent the same as or more than they did while working.

language that will answer your questions about retirement.

Checklists and charts make it easy to pinpoint areas of major concern or interest. *Ready or Not* can be your guide to making the most of what can be the best years of your life, years in which you can take time to truly appreciate your family, your friends, travel, hobbies, or just giving back to your community through volunteering.

Retiring Well

Many couples enter retirement without understanding each other's retirement dreams. Nor do they discuss openly what adjustments they expect to make when their partner retires. This is the time to see if you share the same retirement ideas and to take time for a reality check to plan a happy retirement. The age at which each of you will retire determines how much money you'll need.

It's especially important to discuss and plan the impact of retirement on your spouse and children, and, if you're not married, with your close relatives and friends. Retirement should be about retiring to something, not retiring from something. Planning together will result in days filled with purpose and meaning. It's retiring well.

Aging Gracefully

Every important phase of your life has been successful in proportion to the time and care you have invested: from education to career to marriage and family.

Surprises are fun for parties, but in daily life, as in business, surprises are usually not good news.

The first step to enjoying retirement is to take a close personal inventory.

- How is my health? Regular checkups and early attention to potential problems can save you money and give you more years of active, healthy living.

- Am I financially ready for retirement? A realistic look at your financial situation is crucial. Discuss finances openly with your family. Financial planning is easier if it's shared.

- What will I do in retirement? This is where preparation really pays off. Whether you plan to travel extensively, spend more time with family and friends, get involved in the community, master a new skill, or get a degree, the door of opportunity is wide open. Planning for retirement can let you enjoy leisure as never before.

- Can I still contribute to society? Your experience and acquired knowledge make you invaluable to any number of social, religious and/or civic organizations...and you have the time!

Retirement Options

The concept of 65 as a retirement age appeared when the average American could not expect to live that long. Our literature tells us that 50 was old age into the 1930s.

We are not only living longer, but youthful vigor and mental activity are also being extended.

Retirement income may not be sufficient in itself to meet your needs, whether they are financial or lifestyle-related. Many retirees find alternative work options, from working at home to part-time or flex-time work situations. (See Second Careers, page 84.)

A Winning Attitude

Professional athletes know that the difference between winning and losing usually comes down to attitude. Expect the best from yourself and you're likely to exceed your expectations.

The smart athlete who's "lost a step" learns to anticipate, to stay ahead of the game. Successful retirement means you've stayed ahead by planning—looking clearly and honestly at the future, your personal inventory of resources, your health, and your goals and desires.

"I've got all the money I'll ever need, if I die by four o'clock."

—Henny Youngman

"Inflation is when you pay fifteen dollars for the ten-dollar haircut you used to get for five dollars when you had hair."

—Sam Ewing, humorist

Your Financial Future

Where do you stand? Are you a young person just entering the business world? At the midpoint of your career? Rapidly approaching retirement? Whatever your situation, it makes good sense to regularly and thoroughly review your financial status and do some sound and intensive planning for the future. This chapter will help you do just that. A rich, rewarding life doesn't happen by accident. Whatever your personal/family goals, the best means of achieving them is through planning: financial, career...all aspects of life. It is never too late to start planning.

Planning Is Vital

Without planning, family funds may be spent in a thoughtless and wasteful way. There's never much left for savings and investment, and necessary but perhaps careless borrowing burdens us with expensive interest.

A careless approach to family finances makes life more difficult. There are always major financial needs looming that may further complicate matters: the need for a new furnace, a new car or a new house; children and their own special needs—often costly ones, particularly college educations; and finally, too soon, retirement—often 15 to 20 years of living without that full monthly paycheck.

Note: As you are planning your financial future, be aware that there may be changes in legislation that will affect your assets. Keep informed and check with your financial planner or tax advisor.

Inflation's Impact

Inflation is an insidious thing. We know it is happening, but we don't give sufficient attention to the effect it has on every dollar we earn and save. In the 20-year period from 1998 to 2018, according to the Consumer Price Index, the value of your dollar decreased 54%. If you withdraw $1,000 a month for expenses, after 10 years of 4% inflation, your monthly withdrawal of $1,000 would have the buying power of $675.56, a 34% plunge.

Inflation is a threat to your retirement lifestyle. Inflation reduces the value of your dollar. You will have to consider this in your financial planning, particularly if you are living on a fixed income.

Two Keys to Planning

A sound financial plan is crucial to ensure comfortable living for you and yours, as a safeguard against personal needs, crises and inflation.

This chapter outlines how to develop such a plan, focusing on two important elements:

- Controlling family expenditures by evaluating current spending practices and developing a practical and effective family budget program.

- Ensuring an adequate level of future income by setting up a consistent, diversified and balanced investment plan.

Note: At the end of this chapter, you will find worksheets for computing your cash flow and net worth.

The First Step

The first step is to start developing a personal financial plan. It is important to determine your current financial status so that you can develop a long-range plan to help achieve your financial goals. Primarily this involves computing your net worth. Your net worth is simply the difference between your assets and your liabilities.

Your Net Worth

This computation tells you whether or not your assets (cash, bank accounts, stock, etc.) exceed your liabilities (mortgage, charge cards, etc.)—and by how much. It also tells you the percentage of the total value of your assets that is represented by each category. It provides you with a similar analysis of your liabilities.

With this information, you can evaluate your current financial condition in a systematic way. Review the figures, asking the questions:

- Do I have a major financial problem, with my assets barely exceeding my liabilities?

- Is my life insurance adequate for my family's needs?

- Do I have sufficient money set aside in liquid funds for our current needs?

- Are my investments properly planned and diversified?

- Can I depend on being paid the full value of my loans?

Similar questions should be asked about the composition of liabilities you have listed. They represent, in most instances, heavy finance charges that should be minimized as much and as quickly as possible.

Papers You'll Need

To start, gather all financial papers and reports that provide information on your assets and liabilities. These will include such items as: savings records, checkbooks, statements for CDs, stocks, bonds, funds, etc., and similar reports on your residence, vehicles, mortgages, loans, etc.

You should have all these papers put aside in one place and organized for easy reference. If they are not so organized, this is an opportunity to correct the situation for future reference.

It's not that hard to locate the market value of some of the listed items. Tax reports and records can be helpful, and a check of the classified section of your local paper can give you a good idea of the value of such assets as your home, your cars, tools and equipment, etc.

Richer...or Poorer?

It is a good idea to perform a net worth computation yearly, so that you can see how your net worth is growing. In evaluating this growth, look for two things:

- A steady growth from year to year.

- A growth rate that exceeds the inflation rate by a substantial amount.

If the growth rate is low or uneven, compare this current year's net worth computation alongside last year's and determine any areas of weakness. How are your investments growing in value? Your real estate? Are your liabilities being reduced? Your loan indebtedness? Mortgage obligations?

Effective use of the net worth computation and trend analysis is an important first step in gaining a better understanding of your family's financial condition.

Your Cash Flow

If a look at your net worth (and the trend in its growth—or decline) suggests something needs to be done to improve your financial status, the best way to get a precise understanding of the problem is to compare your *expenses* with your *income* in a specific way. The worksheet for computing your cash flow (page 25) will help you do this.

Determining your cash flow shows you whether or not your expenses exceed your income—or vice versa. If expenses exceed income and you are losing ground financially, obviously you need to take corrective action. If, on the other hand, expenses and income balance out, then the question is whether or not sufficient funds are being set aside for savings and investment.

However, let's assume that the totals as shown clearly indicate you are overspending. You will need to look at the individual items in your "expenses" listing to determine areas in which the spending problem is centered. Probably these areas will stand out like a sore thumb.

Spending Patterns

It is very helpful to compare the percentage of income you spend on each category with a break-down of the following budget for the average retired couple (source: the Bureau of Labor Statistics):

Housing	32%
Transportation	16%
Food	14%
Medical Care	13%
Charity	7%
Insurance/Pension	5%
Entertainment & Education	4%
Clothing	3%
Personal Care	1%
Other	5%

If your percentages vary widely from the table above, this is another clue to the categories in which you may be overspending.

Determining Cash Flow

This takes some doing. Give yourself adequate time to do the job right.

Use the "expenses" listing on the form as your initial guide, taking one category at a time to find the needed information. Much of this information can be obtained from your checkbook, your credit card statements or your tax records.

The most difficult information to get involves cash purchases. Either estimate these figures from personal experience or keep a journal on these items for several weeks to establish a spending pattern.

Income information should be detailed in a similar way, using your income statements for reference purposes.

Important: Don't expect to achieve perfect accuracy with this analysis. Even an imperfect job will give you a strong starting point for understanding and improving your financial status.

What Next?

If you have just completed the Cash Flow Worksheet, you know whether your expenses exceed your income. If they do, you need to take some immediate action to correct this imbalance and start saving for the future.

Even if your income exceeds expenses, it's still a good idea to evaluate and control family spending practices. Do this conscientiously, and use the extra funds to further beef up your savings and investments.

Cutting back on expenses is not as difficult as you might think. Most of us have let items once considered luxuries become necessities. This becomes apparent if we closely study the different elements of our expenses. A $20 savings here—$10 there—an occasional $40–$50 savings, can add up to $150 to $250 monthly, a tidy sum to help in the balancing process.

Examine Your Spending

Look at your listing of expenses. The list covers practically all the ways you can spend your hard-earned income. So take each category; study it carefully—one item at a time.

Take plenty of time, and thoroughly evaluate the expenditures made for each item. Be sure to ask yourself the right questions:

■ Is this product or service really essential?

■ Is there a less expensive version of the item?

- Are we using more of the product or service than we really need?
- Are we buying at a good, competitive price?

Your Action Plan

Follow your review with a written action plan. As you study each category, decide what, if any, reduction plan you want to implement and note it under the appropriate heading in the action plan.

Obviously, you can't implement all reductions at once; so prioritize reductions, putting the most significant first in line. Set a deadline for completion of each one. This puts some pressure on you to make your plan work.

Start taking the actions called for, handling one item at a time. As you complete each action, cross it off your list.

When you have completed this balancing of your expenses and income, you will be ready for the next step—setting up your budget.

A Cooperative Project

You will probably find that many of the expense-reduction measures you decide upon will not penalize anyone in the family. However, if your financial condition is seriously out of balance, more drastic measures must be taken. The decisions reached should be agreed upon with good humor by both partners, with the rest of the family also having input.

Mortgage Savings

As with all budget items, look for ways to save money. With mortgage payments, check current interest rates and see if you can save, taking into account closing costs.

Interest rates have been bouncing around for the past year or so. It may be possible to refinance—lowering the interest rate you're paying. Sure, there will be costs involved in the switch, but in the long run you may be able to save thousands of dollars on interest charges.

You can save money on your mortgage by paying ahead. (See box.) And, are you getting the right coverage and a good price on your homeowner's insurance?

Take a closer look at your insurance policy, and be sure you understand all the provisions and coverages. Check on whether or not they provide the protection you want: not too little, but not too much either—that's costly. Check with a number of insurance companies and compare what the policy will cover and the cost. You might be able to save some money on the premiums.

Carefully check the other house expenditures you make. Maybe you could learn to do more of the little odd jobs yourself.

Make notes on these matters in your expense-reduction action plan.

Note: If you take every category in your listing of expenses and go through them in this way, you can be sure of this: Unless you were the neighborhood's greatest efficiency expert, you will find a lot of savings possibilities that will help you do your balancing act without fear or pain.

MORTGAGE MATH

Here is an example of the difference between a monthly payment and a monthly payment with an additional monthly payment toward the principal on a 30-year $50,000 mortgage at 5% interest.

	Monthly	Extra Payment*
Payment	$268	$100
Annually	$3,221	$4,416
Total interest paid until maturity	$46,628	$23,854
Years to maturity	30 yrs	16 yrs, 9 mos

*It must be written on the check that the additional payment is toward the principal. Check to make sure you can prepay your mortgage.

Set Up a Budget

If you have been developing a financial plan along the lines we have been suggesting, you have examined your spending habits, planned projected adjustments in that spending pattern and set up, in effect, a yearly spending budget by category.

Put this planned spending pattern in a budget form that you can use to control your spending and achieve your financial goals.

Why a Budget?

Besides the obvious advantages of eliminating waste and controlling expenditures, there are a number of additional advantages to living by a budget:

- Having a budget makes the task of achieving financial security much easier. It is a road map, helping you reach your objective with fewer delays and wrong turns.

- You know where you stand financially from month to month.

- It helps generate money for that all-important investment program that will enable you to meet major expenses down the line (home, children, college, retirement).

Some Overall Tips

Many people give up on budgets because they don't use good judgment in setting them up in the first place. To avoid this, consider the following suggestions outlined by many financial planners:

- Continue to approach your working budget as a family project with both partners—and children, too—having input. If decisions are not made on a truly mutual and fair basis, family members just won't work to make the project succeed.

- Keep the budget format—and the necessary administration of the program—as simple as possible. As you go along, you may find ways to eliminate unnecessary details or recordkeeping. Don't forget your primary objective—and the importance of knowing where you stand.

- Accept the first few months as a trial-and-error period. Evaluate what you are doing carefully—making necessary adjustments in allocations and in the way you keep records.

Keeping Budget Records

Standard budget books, as well as budget software packages, are available at every office supply store. Many of them are well-designed, and

instructions for their use are spelled out in detail. Select the one that suits your style. One feature in particular to look for is a thorough breakdown and listing of the various possible types of expenditures. You need such a listing so that you will know which accounts to charge for the wide variety of expenses you incur.

You can also use the format from the "Cash Flow Worksheet" in this section to set up your budget record on a columnar pad. However, it's a good idea to refer to one of the standard books in setting up the category listings, the method of recording information, and the structure for summarizing expenditures.

Your Spending: Keep Track

Whichever budget book you select, the format of the monthly record will be reasonably self-explanatory. There should be a set of instructions on how to make the necessary entries and computations. However, here are a few suggestions that may further simplify the process for you.

- If you look at the budget accounts, you will see it is very easy to obtain much of the information asked for. It is shown either in your checkbook record or credit card statement. Transfer the appropriate information to your budget record once a month. Recognize the value of a checkbook record as a source of budget information.

- Other expenses include cash purchases for food, entertainment, personal care, etc. Some plan must be set up to keep track of these expenditures. One way is to keep receipts for all cash purchases, checking to be sure they clearly show the items purchased and the prices paid.

- Where no receipt is provided, keep a listing in a notebook you carry for that purpose. With these notes, it is easy to update your budget record.

- Another control on small-item purchases is the business Purchase Order approach. Establish a limit on an item, such as meals out, and limit spending to that level. Try this, and you'll

watch your nickels and dimes. This makes it easy to record the total of these expenditures in your budget book. The amount spent should be the amount budgeted—or less.

Your Budget at Work

Keeping your budget program working is the last and most important step in the process. This starts with a clear assignment of responsibilities.

- Who is going to be responsible for keeping the budget records? This must be specified so that the job gets done regularly.

- How is responsibility for controlling different categories of spending to be divided between household partners? Cash purchases of food, entertainment, personal care and miscellaneous items are a particular problem here. You should look at this matter together, using recent experience as your guide, and make a list of the specific items for which each will be responsible.

Where to Keep Your Money

Where do you keep the budget funds so they are safe yet readily available? Some people choose a joint checking account; others choose a savings account *and* a checking account. Separate checking accounts are a third way. With this system, an appropriate allocation of monthly income is made to each account to cover assigned expenditures. Each spouse draws on their account as needed during the month, for cash or to pay current bills by check. Whatever system you decide on, make the plan concrete and follow the agreed-upon procedure to avoid any misunderstanding.

Finally, there is the very important monthly budget review. This review determines whether or not your program works. At this review, you and your partner check whether or not you are staying within budget limits. If not, decide what action to take to stop overspending—account by account. If you are underspending in some categories, you can adjust upward the budget limits in other account categories as good judgment advises.

A budget program as outlined here will provide reasonable assurance that you are spending your income wisely and in line with your preferences. Also, if you have planned well, you will know that allocations are being made regularly to your investment account, to ensure continued financial security.

Investing

We now move ahead to another important phase of our financial planning. We have set aside funds for savings and investments of some kind. The amount in your budget for this purpose may be small, but hopefully it will increase as you add a portion of your future cost-of-living and merit pay increases to the funds designated for savings.

You need to develop a plan for utilizing these funds effectively. Such a plan should provide for current day-to-day living expenses, minimize credit card and loan debt, and make a start on setting aside money for major family requirements such as: home, children, advanced education and, ultimately, retirement.

This section covers the alternatives available for such savings and investment purposes and how to structure such a program. There are three phases

Investing Through the Years			
Invest Each Month	Starting at Age	Total Invested	Total Value at Age 65
$200	35	$72,000	$166,452
400	35	144,000	332,903
200	45	48,000	82,206
400	45	96,000	164,413
200	55	24,000	31,056
400	55	48,000	62,113

Figures are approximate based on annual return of investments of 5%. Factors to consider are taxes and inflation. Investments in a Roth IRA can be withdrawn tax-free.

in line with the way such a program is realistically developed:

- First phase: setting aside an adequate working fund and essential insurance protection.

- Second phase: starting a savings program to provide added financial protection and coverage of future needs.

- Third phase: developing a full-blown savings and investment plan.

Just in Case...

As the heading suggests, at the start of your financial planning, you should take care of two prime financial needs: a working fund and insurance protection. We'll begin with…

The Working Fund

Every family needs such a fund. It provides for your day-to-day expenses and also should be large enough to cover major expenses such as car repairs, all but the largest appliance purchases, and even emergencies such as a temporary lay-off. These funds should be readily available. Still, even at this first stage, you want this fund to be earning *something* in the form of interest.

The problem of credit card and other debt appears at this point. Some people seem to think that having a credit card—or two or more—somehow *increases* their income. Of course, it doesn't—just the opposite. Rather than saving you money, it costs you a whopping 12–27% in interest each year. Yet the use of a credit card for borrowing purposes becomes a habit. The required monthly payment seems small, and more and more debt accumulates.

Credit Card Dangers

This is a dangerous financial situation. It has become a real problem for you when you start to see tell-tale signs such as these: You never have adequate funds to start paying down the balance on your credit cards. You must use a credit card to borrow money to meet day-to-day living expenses. You take out a new credit card to borrow money to make the payments on your current cards. (See page 43.)

Here's an example that highlights the folly of using credit cards carelessly:

- Suppose you save $2,000 and put it in a savings account earning 1.5% interest. You will earn $30 per year on your savings.

- Suppose, on the other hand, you put aside $2,000 and paid off the $2,000 balance on your credit card. You would save—in effect, earn—18% on the transaction, or $360. That's $280 more than the $80 you would earn on $2,000 in a 4% savings account.

The rule of thumb is to never use credit to pay for everyday living expenses. Use credit to buy assets that have long-term value: a home, a car, a major appliance that reduces living expenses.

Back to the working fund. Obviously such a fund helps you avoid excessive credit card and loan indebtedness. The question is: How much should you have in such a fund? Financial planners seem to agree you should keep about three to six months of income in such a fund. That is:

- With a $2,500 monthly income: a fund of $7,500–$15,000

- With a $3,500 monthly income: a fund of $10,500–$21,000

As to where you keep these funds, the alternatives are probably familiar to you and are mostly available from your local bank or credit union. Make sure these savings alternatives guarantee security of your funds either by the FDIC or the NCUA and your account totals less than the stipulated limit for liability.

Structuring Your Savings

The purpose of starting a savings and investment program is to provide financial security as the

How Long Will Your Money Last?

This chart shows you how long your capital will last if you withdraw a fixed amount each year.

Percentage Withdrawn Yearly	Years Money Will Last If Invested at These Rates:					
	5%	6%	7%	8%	9%	10%
4%	*	*	*	*	*	*
8%	21	24	31	*	*	*
10%	15	16	18	21	27	*
12%	11	12	13	15	17	19
14%	10	10	11	12	12	14
16%	8	9	9	10	10	11
18%	7	7	8	8	9	9
20%	6	7	7	7	7	8

* means it will last indefinitely at that rate.

The goal is to have your money last as long as you do. Your budget should be able to respond to changes in investment performance, life expectancy and other factors.

years go by—particularly in retirement. As we have emphasized, inflation makes this a particularly difficult goal to achieve.

Keep just enough in your checking to meet current monthly needs and the rest in the money management account, earning interest. Watch closely the balance between accounts to be sure you are earning interest on as much of your fund as possible.

Insurance Protection

If you're married and have a family, you must realize the need for insurance protection, in the event some unforeseen tragedy should befall you or your spouse. This need is greatest when you are younger, as the insurance benefit must provide income for your family over many years. As you grow older, your policy will provide liquidity for your estate or pay your estate taxes.

Over the years, you should build assets that provide income protection. Set up your life insurance program *early* as part of your financial base.

The type of money managers you and your spouse are determines, to a great extent, the type of insurance plan that is best for you. (See box.)

How Much Protection?

Few people can afford to buy sufficient insurance protection to guarantee that their families will not suffer a loss of income at the death or disability of the major wage earner. Instead, do the best you can with the money available for this purpose.

The first thing to do is to consider what income the family would have, considering such factors as: earning ability of the surviving spouse, the current state of the family finances, children's education, and the possibility and level of Social Security benefits. Set up your insurance plan to come as close as possible to the monthly income needed for reasonably comfortable living.

Disability Insurance

You're twice as likely to be disabled for 90 days as to die before age 65. Yet fewer than half of all working adults have disability insurance.

You and your spouse need enough coverage to maintain 60% to 70% of your current family income if either of you become disabled. Group coverage through your employer is cheapest. If that's not available, try to get a group rate through a group to which you belong.

The older you are when you apply for disability insurance, the higher the cost. You can lower costs by stretching the elimination period. A policy that starts payments on Day 90 of disability will cost 40% less than one that pays on Day 30.

Cash Value Life Insurance

The newer forms of life insurance—variable life, for example—have better investment potential than whole life policies, assuming the investments do well. So, should you consider switching? While there are cost and legal implications, a better question is: Do you still need the insurance, and is that need likely to last for your lifetime?

As you grow older, what remains is the cash value, or the investment. Investing in an insurance policy is expensive. Agent commissions, state premium taxes, required reserves and so forth all reduce the investment. And none are present in, say, no-load mutual funds. Other things being equal, lower costs mean greater returns.

After 11–16 years, your policy should be paid up and there will be sufficient cash value to pay the premium for the remainder of the policy.

INSURANCE OPTIONS

Term Insurance provides the greatest dollar amount of coverage for the least amount of money— $100,000 of protection for just several hundred dollars per year. However, the premiums for a specific amount of insurance become greater as you grow older. Term insurance does not build any cash value.

Whole Life Insurance provides a stipulated death benefit, but it also includes a savings feature, building cash value as the years go by. You can borrow against this cash value and, if you eventually cancel the policy, cash it in, obtaining the savings that have built up. The chief problem with this type of policy is the low rate of interest usually earned in the savings phase of the plan. (Universal life invests a portion in a term policy and another portion to a side fund upon which interest is paid.)

Variable Life Insurance combines the features of a whole life policy with those of a mutual fund. Be careful before purchasing. There are commissions, annual charges, penalties for early withdrawal and severance fees in many of the policies. Understand the policy, and check with your financial planner or accountant. There is a risk that your premium will be increased and your death benefits will not be guaranteed. Resist high-pressure sales pitches.

Building a Retirement Fund

Let's look at two examples of how a retirement fund can build over the years through the magic of compound interest. You will note that in addition to the regular contributions to the plan, all earnings are also reinvested as the years go by.

Looking at these two examples, you can see that even a relatively modest amount of monthly savings can quickly grow into a substantial fund that can provide added income in your retirement years. A few added points of interest on your investments can substantially increase the growth of such a fund.

In considering these examples, you must remember that the results shown do not reflect the effect of any income tax requirements, a factor which could severely effect the growth in appreciation shown. This calls attention to the value of an investment approach that takes advantage of any tax-free or tax-deferred investments available.

Every person or family should have some type of savings or investment program. It may involve only a modest contribution, but these contributions are made consistently into a carefully selected, tax-efficient investment that provides a decent return and appreciation.

When you talk about setting up a savings and investment program, you discover people fall into two categories:

- They work for a business or other type of organization.
- They are self-employed.

Let's consider the investment approach appropriate to each of these groups.

Working for a Business

There are two approaches you can use to make your beginning savings and investment program tax-efficient:

- Participation in company retirement program.
- Use of an individual retirement account (IRA).

Your Employer's Program

Employer retirement programs vary widely, but a typical program might very well include: life, accident and disability insurance; a non-contributory and a contributory pension plan; a cash balance plan; a company savings and stock investment plan; and more.

The advantages of such employer programs are numerous, including the fact that they provide the tax-efficient approach that is so important to decent growth in your investment savings. This applies to both simplified employee pension (SEP) and 401(k) plans. In some instances, your initial contributions to these plans are excluded from your earnings before income taxes are withheld. Usually earnings on all types of contributions are sheltered from income taxes while they are held in the plan and until they are withdrawn.

In addition to the tax advantages of such a plan, employer contributions often make the plans doubly attractive. The employer usually covers many of the required program costs: the noncontributory part of the pension plan, the full cost of some phases of the insurance program, a sizable percentage add-on for every dollar saved and invested by an employee participant (half a dollar or more in many instances). Just think:

A modest $200 monthly contribution to the employer 401(k) program may qualify for a $100 or more matching contribution by the employer for a total of $300 monthly—$3,600 per year.

Because of the advantages of your employer program, you should make every effort to participate using the funds set aside in your budget for such a program.

Pension Protection Act

The Pension Protection Act of 2006 requires employers to allow participants in defined contribution plans that are invested in employer securities to elect to direct the plan to divest employer securities into other investment options.

Employers are now allowed to automatically enroll their employees into a 401(k)-type plan with default contribution levels. Employees can opt out at any time. Employers can now offer a Roth 401(k) plan. An employee can choose to designate some or all of their permissible contributions to either plan. Unlike the regular 401(k), in a Roth 401(k) you pay tax on the money you contribute but none on the money you take out. You do not get a tax deduction for contributing to a Roth 401(k). A Roth 401(k) may have higher administration fees.

The beneficiaries of the retirement plan can now roll over assets inherited into an IRA.

Lump-Sum Distributions

If you have participated in a 401(k) or any other qualified retirement plan for three years, you may have the option of receiving a lump-sum distribution upon leaving employment. If your plan has a balance of $1,000 to $5,000, your employer will deposit this directly into an IRA unless otherwise directed.

Choosing the lump sum is not the best decision. Before taking the lump sum in cash, you should consider your life expectancy and the potential needs of your surviving spouse. A lump-sum distribution is usually the entire balance in your retirement savings plan. Since this could be a large sum, you should consult a tax advisor to help you decide among the available options.

Basically, you can take the distribution as ordinary income and pay taxes on it the year it is received (no tax is due on your after-tax contributions). Or, you can defer taxation by rolling over all or part of the money into an individual retirement account (IRA). Other alternatives for your distribution include: keeping it invested in stock, buying an individual retirement annuity, or leaving it in your employer's plan.

In determining the best course of action, consider the amount of the distribution, how soon you need the money, other resources available to you, your age, your health, your family, and anticipated investment returns.

Option 1: Take Cash

You have the option to take the entire lump sum in cash. **This is not the best option.** Taxes must be paid on the amount received (excluding any after-tax contributions). If you are under $59^{1}/_{2}$, you may incur a 10% penalty for early withdrawal.

YOUR EMPLOYER'S RETIREMENT PROGRAM: FACTORS TO CONSIDER

■ Study the employer retirement brochure carefully to be sure you understand all the benefits available to you. Study the details, too, so you know the key rights and restrictions pertaining to each of these benefits. For example, there probably will be restrictions or penalties for withdrawal from the fund. On the other hand, you may be able to borrow against your investments in an emergency and avoid such penalties.

■ Consider the savings funds you have available monthly, and carefully select the type of investments you prefer. Perhaps you start with participation in the contributory phase of the pension plan, an approach which earns good returns and helps ensure that your basic pension at retirement is ample for your needs. You might put any additional funds available in the 401(k) plan. **Be careful.** It is unwise to have all of your 401(k) investment in your employer's stock. Diversify.

■ A number of employers are adopting cash balance pension plans instead of traditional pension programs. These plans are advantageous to younger workers who may change jobs frequently and can take a lump-sum payment when they leave the employer. Employers also save money. For older workers, unless the company continues them in the old plan, as many do, there is a significant drop in pension benefits. Check your plan.

Feature Comparisons of Retirement Accounts			
Feature	**Designated Roth 401(k)**	**Roth IRA**	**Traditonal 401(k)**
Contributions	Designated Roth employee elective contributions are made with *after-tax dollars*.	Roth IRA contributions are made with *after-tax dollars*.	Traditional, pre-tax employee elective contributions are made with *pre-tax dollars*.
Income Limits	No income limitation to participate.	Income limits: Married phaseout starts at $193,000 to ineligible at $203,000. Single phaseout starts at $122,000 to ineligible at $137,000 (modified AGI).	No income limitation to participate.
Maximum Elective Contributions	Combined* employee elective contributions limited to: $19,000 ($25,000 for employees 50 or over).	Contribution limited to: $6,000 ($7,000 for employees 50 or over).	Same combined* limit as designated Roth 401(k) account.
Taxation Withdrawals	Withdrawals of contributions and earnings are not taxed provided they are a qualified distribution—account is held for at least 5 years and made: because of disability, or death or after attainment of age 59½.	Same as designated Roth 401(k) account; and can have a qualified distribution for a first-time home purchase.	Withdrawals of contributions and earnings are subject to federal and most state income taxes.
Required Distributions	Distributions must begin no later than age 70½, unless still working and not a 50% owner.	No requirement to start taking distributions while owner is alive.	Same as designated Roth 401(k) account.

*This limitation is by individual, rather than by plan. Although permissible to split the annual employee elective contribution between designated Roth contributions and traditional pre-tax contributions, the combination cannot exceed the deferral limit.

Source: IRS

Employers must withhold 20% from eligible rollover distributions for federal income taxes unless the money is directly rolled over to an IRA or another qualified retirement plan.

You may be able to minimize your tax bite. It becomes complicated. Consult with a tax accountant before you take the money.

Option 2: Roll Over Into an IRA

You can defer paying income taxes on all or part of a lump-sum distribution by reinvesting the money in an IRA through a direct or indirect rollover. (After-tax contributions made after 2001 can be transferred.)

In order to avoid having 20% of your distribution withheld, you should request a direct rollover to an IRA (Trust to Trust). With this approach, you instruct your employer to directly roll your distribution into an IRA rather than pay the money to you. Make sure it is payable to the custodian of your new IRA. Otherwise, the distribution will be subject to the 20% withholding and maybe penalties.

If the distribution is paid to you, you can still do an indirect rollover in which you have 60 days to reinvest the money in an IRA. However, even if you roll over the total amount received, you will pay income taxes, as well as a possible 10% penalty if you're under age 59½, on the 20% of the distribution withheld by your employer. To avoid this, you must roll over the 20% from your own pocket.

With this option, you must begin to take your required minimum distribution, determined by the IRS, at age 70½.

Option 3: Keep the Stock

If your retirement plan consists mostly of highly appreciated stock, it might be a good idea to keep the stock. You will owe taxes, but only on the value of the shares at the time you purchased them or when the company added them to your account. You can continue to defer taxes on all the share-price gains from the initial date of purchase until you sell the stock. You will pay annual income taxes on any dividends.

In doing this, you convert what might have been ordinary income into long-term capital gain. Your heirs may fare better with this option since they will owe taxes only on the share-price gain of the stock prior to taking the shares out of the plan.

To find out how much you might save in taxes, ask your employee benefits department to provide

FINDING LOST PENSIONS

Are you due a pension, but your old employer has gone out of business and you don't know where to go to collect your money? Help is available from:

www.pbgc.gov
Click on "Have an Unclaimed Pension?"

The Pension Benefit Guaranty Corporation
Pension Search Program
P.O. Box 151750
Alexandria, VA 22315-1750

800 400-7242 • mypension@pbgc.gov

Include:

- Name & Address
- Daytime telephone number
- Social Security number
- Date of birth
- Name and location of the employer
- Dates of employment

Also, if you have any documents issued by the plan, include the nine-digit Employer Identification Number and the three-digit Plan Identification Number that are often printed on such papers.

you with the net unrealized appreciation (NUA) on those shares before you make any withdrawals.

Keep in mind that the principle underlying good retirement planning is **diversification**. Do not put all your eggs in one basket. Although you will get favorable tax treatment by keeping company stock, it must not be the overriding consideration.

Option 4: Take a Lifetime Annuity

Many plans offer annuity distributions. Should you desire an annuity, it's probably a better value to obtain one through your employer's plan. Annuities are complicated. **Be careful!** Some offer advantages, while others should not be purchased. There are sales commissions, fees and charges that vary widely and affect your return. Should you withdraw within a certain period, usually up to seven years, most annuities have severance charges. For a withdrawal before 59½, under most circumstances, there will be a 10% penalty on the interest you have earned. Learn all you can about annuities before purchasing.

Option 5: Employer's Plan

You may choose to leave the lump sum in your employer's plan. Check with your plan administrator. If they allow former participants to keep their accounts, the likely result is lower cost and thus higher returns. Remember, if you roll over your lump sum, you become an individual investor and may encounter charges such as fees and commissions, two things normally not present in the employer's plan. **Be careful.** If your employer's plan is heavily invested in your employer's stock, it is wise to diversify. But be aware that investments may be moved without your permission.

Option 6: New Employment

If you switch employment from a nonprofit or government job to the private sector or vice versa, the 2001 Tax Act allows you to roll your tax-deferred retirement savings vehicles, including 403(b) plans, some 457 plans or traditional IRAs, to your new employer's retirement plan.

Individual Retirement Account

If your employer does not have a retirement program, you will want to make an IRA your first choice for the investment of your retirement savings. Even if you do have a company program, you probably will want to participate to the extent possible under the terms of the IRA plan—if you have the funds to do so.

Any of several different investments can be used for an IRA account. In setting up and participating in such a program, you will want to do your homework and base your decision on sound research and good judgment.

Traditional & Roth IRA

- Contributions to a traditional IRA are tax-deductible in the year they are made, and taxes are owed on distributions. Roth IRA contributions are not tax-deductible but withdrawals are tax-free.

- The annual contribution limit is $6,000.

- For those who attain the age of 50, the maximum annual amount is $7,000. You must have earned income to cover your contribution.

- Beneficiaries may roll over retirement plan balances to their own retirement plan or traditional IRA.

- With the Roth IRA, contributions can be withdrawn without taxes or penalties after the account has been open 5 years and after age 59½ or for death, disability, higher education or certain home purchases.

- With the traditional IRA, a tax-deferred plan, there is a 10% penalty for withdrawal prior to age 59½, except in the case of death, disability, higher education or certain home purchases.

- With a traditional IRA, you must start taking your required minimum distribution, determined by the IRS, no later than April 1 of the year after you turn 70½. In a Roth IRA, you never have to withdraw your money. This can help in estate planning, since a Roth IRA will allow you to leave tax-sheltered money to your heirs and avoid taking your required minimum distribution, determined by the IRS.

SIMPLE SAVINGS STEPS...

- Take advantage of your pension plan, payroll deduction plan, 401(k) salary deduction plan and/or deferred compensation plan.

- Have a separate savings account.

- Do not spend your next raise.

- If you get a tax refund or bonus, save it.

- Pay off your mortgage sooner by making extra payments on the principal.

- Pay off credit cards to save the money you now spend on interest charges.

- Ask to have all dividends from mutual funds or stocks automatically reinvested.

- Contribute to an IRA.

- Save early. Thanks to compounding, $1,000 saved this year will have far greater value when you retire than the same $1,000 put away 10 or 20 years from now.

- Trim your spending.

- If you have a company 401(k) and you have separated from service with that company during or after you reach age 55, there will be no penalty for taking distributions from the plan. This does not apply to IRA accounts. To maintain this penalty-free distribution, the funds must not be rolled over into an IRA. **Make sure** you understand all the rules before starting a distribution, since it could result in costly mistakes. Also take into consideration how you will fund your many years in retirement.

- Anyone can convert their traditional IRA to a Roth IRA. When you convert from an IRA to a Roth IRA, you owe ordinary income tax on the converted amount. You should have enough money to pay the tax with other funds. If you pay with the funds in the IRA, it would be considered a premature distribution subject to a 10% penalty.

If You Are Self-Employed

You can take advantage of the tax-efficient benefits of what is called a Keogh plan. This plan is similar to an IRA but is designed specifically for persons who work for themselves: doctors, dentists, store owners, accountants, freelance writers, etc. Sole proprietors and partners may set up a Keogh plan. There are certain legal requirements. You may want to see an accountant.

A tax deduction for contributions to a retirement plan and deferral of tax on income to the plan are benefits that apply to all self-employed persons (including owner-employees) who have a Keogh plan. The amount eligible for deduction is substantial, but the formula varies with the specific type of Keogh plan involved.

Balanced Approach

As mentioned under the discussion of IRAs, you will probably—at the start—want to take a balanced approach to your investments. Here are several types you may consider because they provide reasonable safety and security and usually provide an improved rate of earnings over savings accounts.

Certificates of Deposit. Traditional certificates of deposit (CDs) are available at banks and savings and loan institutions and have a long-standing reputation as low-risk investments. CDs offer higher interest rates than regular savings accounts and can be easily converted to cash. The investor may withdraw the principal before the CD matures by paying a modest penalty.

Some new breeds of CDs from brokerage firms are very different. Some have variable interest rates. Some take decades to mature. Some give the brokerage firm the right to terminate the CD but do not give that right to the investor. If the investor needs money before the CD matures, the only option is to sell the CD back to the broker, often at a significant loss.

For more CD information, contact the SEC's Office of Investor Education, U.S. Securities and Exchange Commission, 100 F Street, NE, Washington DC 20549-0213, 800-732-0330, or www.sec.gov.

Bonds and Bond Funds. You can buy and sell individual bonds, but many investors find it less complicated to use mutual bond funds. These funds spread their investments over the bonds of many different companies and governmental organizations, thus providing the security that comes with diversification.

IF YOU DON'T WAIT 'TILL LATER...

IRA TREE PLANTED AT AGE 55

YOUR YIELD WILL BE GREATER

IRA TREE PLANTED AT AGE 35

Bond funds usually are categorized into three groups: corporate, government and tax-free municipals. Overall, they are considered to be relatively low-risk investments, but they do not have guaranteed security in some cases.

Bond funds usually provide an attractive rate of return on your investment. However, the share value of bonds and bond funds, including government bond funds, fluctuates with interest rates: share value goes down when interest rates go up, and share values go up when interest rates go down.

Balanced Mutual Stock Funds and Growth and Income Funds. These funds seek both capital growth and dividend income through balanced investments in both stocks and bonds. They are not as risk-free as certificates of deposit or bond funds, but on average they generally provide a good return on your investments over a period of time.

Whatever type of investment you decide to use, you will want to emphasize certain approaches in carrying out your program.

- Select the funds and sources in which you plan to invest very carefully. That is, comparison shop. Be particularly careful of fees and commissions.

- Make your yearly investment as large as possible, considering the funds you have available.

- Make your contribution procedure as painless as possible by setting it up as an automatic payroll deduction or as an automatic payment from your bank savings account.

Expanding Investments

The purpose of this phase of your investment planning is to increase your savings to the point that they will provide for the additional needs and preferences of the family: advanced education for the children, a better home, the possibility of travel now and in retirement, etc.

Ideally, your personal situation at this point is that your income from work has increased, or perhaps your spouse has gone to work as well.

You continue to live on your budget (somewhat modified, of course) so that funds are not being wasted. Now, you should look beyond the basic start you have made in your employer retirement program, IRA or Keogh plan to a more extensive form of investment.

Sound Investment Program

In approaching your expanded program, you will continue to look for opportunities to reduce the bite of taxation by using a tax-efficient approach, where possible.

There are other important factors to look for:

Prime quality investments: Whether it is a stock fund, a certificate of deposit or a house, explore the alternatives carefully. Comparison shop.

Diversified portfolio: Nobody—even the very best financial planner—is smart enough to call the shots right all the time. Experts agree on one thing: The best way to cut your investment risks is to diversify.

Balanced portfolio: Look for greater potential growth of your investment dollars by including a balance of aggressive, conservative and liquid investment instruments in your portfolio.

Minimum administrative costs: Loads, fees and commissions can cut your investment profits excessively. So, look for no-load, minimum-cost investments and avoid turning over your investments more often than necessary.

Consistency of contributions: As we stated earlier, consistency is an important factor in building a substantial investment fund over the years. This approach has the added advantage of letting you "dollar average" your purchases, a process that tends to hold down the average cost of shares, which continually fluctuate in price.

Stay Tuned to the Economy

We are not suggesting you should attempt to foresee and react to every change of the economic situation. Whether the economic forecast appears to be good or bad for the long run, it should be given major consideration in your investment planning.

In applying these investment principles, there are in general two different approaches to take:

- Do it yourself.
- Use a financial planner.

The Do-It-Yourself Approach

The first step is to do some further study of the investment business generally.

Subscribe to one of the major investment-type publications. It will keep you apprised of changes, trends and prospects in the market. Take courses on the subject of investing at one of your local colleges.

Select a family of funds with a proven track record. Such families include among their offerings a wide variety of mutual stock and bond funds. One big advantage of working with a family is that you get the privilege of moving your investments from one type of fund to another quite freely, often without a special charge for the transaction. This is an important, cost-saving factor when you need to switch from more aggressive funds to more conservative ones because of a change in the economic climate. Make sure your fund expenses are under 1% (see page 46).

Do a thorough comparison check of the various families you are considering. Also check the performance record of these funds as shown in frequent research studies, published regularly in the popular financial monthlies. Then, and only then, make a selection of a family to work with.

Using a Financial Planner

Although financial planners can help you make investment decisions, hiring a planner presumes you have discretionary income to invest. Experts say most investments should not be made until you have financed very basic living items, such as housing, insurance and a cash reserve fund for emergencies. If you find you cannot meet these (and other) necessary financial requirements, you may decide you need help not in investment planning but in basic money management.

Whether or not you use the services of a financial planner, you must organize by preparing your own net-worth and cash-flow worksheets.

Be informed on financial matters. Your local educational institutions offer classes. Do this whether or not you hire a financial planner.

A financial planner should help not only with your investments, including creating a retirement strategy, but also with your insurance and estate planning. Get recommendations from other financial professionals, such as an insurance agent or lawyer, and ask your friends and colleagues. Interview 3 or 4 advisors to find out if they are a good match for you. Be careful. Before choosing a financial planner, ask these four questions:

- What are your qualifications?
- What can you sell me?
- May I talk with other clients like me?
- How do you get paid? (See page 122.)

Balancing Your Portfolio

Selecting the balance you want in your portfolio is another step. You should first consider your attitude toward investment risk. If you invest in stocks and bonds, you are going to have to face the prospect of market downs and ups. The fact is you cannot avoid all risks just by investing conservatively. As an example, a guaranteed savings account will only earn you about 1% on your savings, on which you'll have to pay taxes. The average inflation rate is 4% per year.

An exchange-traded fund (ETF) is a hybrid between a mutual fund and the stocks/bonds themselves. They are a basket of securities that are designed to track one specific index, e.g., Standard & Poor's (S&P) 500, NASDAQ 100, Dow Jones, etc. The benefits are a very low fee, about 18 basis points vs. 140 basis points for a stock fund. The other significant benefit is that you determine when the ETF is sold, so you have control over short- and long-term capital gain. Mutual funds must distribute all their income each year to avoid being a taxable entity. The major disadvantage is you may give up some diversification unless you own a group of ETFs. For example, if you purchase an SPDR, which represents the S&P 500, you have purchased a large cap fund that does not include small and mid-cap, value, growth, international and real estate, to name a few.

There are several additional types of mutual funds that should be given consideration at this stage of your planning. Previously, we described money market funds, certificates of deposit, bonds and bond funds, and balanced funds. There are also:

Aggressive Growth and Long-Term Growth Funds. These mutual stock funds aim for maximum growth in stock value and capital gains while providing dividend income. However,

they involve substantial risks because of their aggressive investment policy, and their share prices may fluctuate widely.

Index Trust. The difficulty of beating the Dow and other market averages has been shown by numerous studies. So the index trust or index mutual stock fund was created. The list of stocks held by such funds is set up to match those included in one of the popular stock indexes (for example, the Standard and Poor's Index). As a result, the share price of the index trust closely follows the downs and ups of the market. Since the overall trend of stock market prices over the long run has been up, this characteristic should be advantageous in the long run.

The purpose of your balancing plan is to set up a portfolio of stocks that will give you, to some extent, the growth potential of aggressive mutual stock funds while retaining a measure of security

SAVING FOR EDUCATION

Planning for college is important, especially since college tuitions are rising. When deciding the best way to save for college, consider a Roth IRA for yourself. You will have flexibility and control over the money. Be sure you keep some funds for your own retirement. Remember, there are grants and loans available for college, but not for your retirement plan. For more information, go to www.savingforcollege.com and collegesavings.org. Consider starting a Roth IRA for the child. The child must have income from a job. You or the child can put up to $6,000 into a Roth IRA or 100% of earned income, whichever is less. *Your contribution would be considered a gift.* The rules for a Roth IRA apply. The child should not withdraw money from the Roth IRA until after the last financial aid form is filed, since it will count as income to the student.

Section 529 College Savings Plans
This tuition program allows you to prepay tuition credits or cash contributions. Anyone can contribute: parents, relatives and friends. You can invest in any state plan, regardless of where you live. Contributions, fees and expenses vary from state to state; some states tax the out-of-state plans. Penalties may apply if the student attends a private or other state school or does not use the money for education. The Pension Protection Act of 2006 provides college savers using 529 plans with tax benefits. If you are a grandparent and the parents have a 529 plan, consider contributing to the parents' account for a child. Money withdrawn from a nonparental 529 plan counts as student income and cuts a need-based aid package up to 50% of the distribution, while only 5.6%, at the most, of a parental plan is counted.

Coverdell Education Savings Account
The maximum yearly contribution is $2,000; all earnings are scheduled to be taxed as ordinary income and subject to a 10% penalty unless the money is used for college expenses. If the account isn't used for education by the time the beneficiary is 30, the proceeds are paid out to the beneficiary and are subject to income tax plus a 10% penalty. You may contribute in the same year for the same student to an education savings account and to a 529 plan.

against market downturns. This is accomplished through the investment of a portion of your savings in aggressive funds, a portion in conservative funds and a portion in liquid investments.

The major fund families promote this approach to investment planning, and you will find recommendations in their brochures for developing your own basic plan.

You can see that the planners' recommendations become more and more weighted toward conservative investments as the investors get older and the need for security of savings becomes greater. Of course, the long-term health of the economy as forecast by the financial community should also be given serious consideration.

Taking Action

Actually setting up your investment program is the final action to take in getting started. Review the stocks available from the family of funds you intend to work with, and make a preliminary selection. Then contact the fund family, discuss your plans for balancing your investment program and the tentative fund selections you have made, and get the counsel of the fund representative.

Plan for Retirement Now

Advance planning for retirement should begin in your 40s, certainly no later than your early to mid-50s.

Now, more than ever before, careful financial planning is necessary to acquire the assets needed to assure a comfortable and happy retirement. This can't be put off until you are 60 or over.

Generally, a combined pension program and Social Security will yield about 60% of your preretirement income. You may be able to live on less after you retire, but you probably will need a supplementary income to avoid a lowered standard of living.

In your 40s and 50s, concentrate on financing retirement years. In your 50s, begin giving more serious thought to what you want in retirement, how you would like to spend your time, where you will live and what adjustments you might have to make. You should think in specific ways about retirement—and if you are married, the planning should be done jointly. In your 50s, you should have a good idea of what you're going to do in your retirement.

In your early 60s, you must begin thinking about when you will retire—at 65? Earlier, with reduced benefits? Or later?

FINANCING YOUR RETIREMENT?

Checklist
✔ for Financial Preparation

Have you—

Yes	No	
❏	❏	Created an adequate working fund whose purpose is to provide money for day-to-day living and help minimize debt?
❏	❏	Obtained a life insurance plan that provides adequate protection at a competitive cost—particularly during early family years?
❏	❏	Made consistent contributions of even modest amounts to a savings and investment program to build up to significant levels over the years?
❏	❏	Used employer retirement programs, such as IRAs and Keogh accounts?
❏	❏	Made a full-blown investment program based on a thorough understanding of the characteristics of a sound program (i.e., need for diversification, balance, etc.), whether you do it yourself or use a reliable financial planner?
❏	❏	Put all your vital financial papers in one place, told someone else where they are and made copies of them?
❏	❏	Figured your retirement expenses, keeping inflation in mind, identified financial assets and projected their growth before retirement?
❏	❏	Talked over retirement finances with your spouse or, if you are single, with someone close to you?
❏	❏	Figured what survivor's benefits you or your spouse would receive if either one of you died?
❏	❏	Obtained investment and savings information and planned for improving your approach to savings and investment for further investigation?
❏	❏	Paid down your credit card debt and paid off your mortgage and car payments?
❏	❏	Built up an emergency fund, i.e., health, pet, fire? Budgeted for capital expenses, i.e., roof, car or painting of house?
❏	❏	Reviewed your expenses and savings at least once a year?

If you checked any item "No," you know where you need to do some work.

Quick Financial Overview

The first step in financial planning is to figure out where you stand today. Take a few moments to fill out this worksheet. Don't spend a lot of time digging through records or being exact. Just make your best estimate for each category. You will want to do a more careful analysis later (see the worksheets on pages 25 and 26). You may be surprised at your financial status. This will give you a basis for your financial and retirement planning.

Monthly Income

Monthly wages; salary	$ _____
Dividends/interest	$ _____
Other	$ _____
TOTAL MONTHLY INCOME	$ _____

Monthly Expenses

Mortgage/rent	$ _____
Transportation	$ _____
Food	$ _____
Education	$ _____
Child Care	$ _____
Entertainment/recreation	$ _____
Loans (car/credit card, etc.)	$ _____
Utilities (gas, phone, electricity, water, etc.)	$ _____
Miscellaneous (clothes, insurance, medical, etc.)	$ _____
TOTAL MONTHLY EXPENSES	$ _____

	Monthly Income	$ _____
(minus)	Monthly Expenses	– $ _____
(plus)	Savings and Investments	+ $ _____
(equals)	**TOTAL DISCRETIONARY CASH**	= $ _____

Retirement Expense Worksheet

STEP 1: Using this worksheet, record everything you spend for one month. If you have some expenses that don't fit any category, include them at the bottom.

STEP 2: To determine your yearly expenses, multiply your monthly expenses by 12.

STEP 3: To determine your projected yearly retirement expenses, multiply your yearly expenses by .90. The result is an approximation of how much you'll need per year during retirement, not factoring in inflation.

Housing (rent or mortgage, property/real estate taxes, household maintenance)	$ _____
Essentials (food, clothing, medical and dental bills)	$ _____
Taxes (income, property and Social Security)	$ _____
Utilities (gas, electric, telephone)	$ _____
Transportation (car loans, gas, car maintenance, plane, train, bus and taxi fares)	$ _____
Leisure (vacation home mortgage, entertainment, travel, club dues)	$ _____
Loan and installment payments (bank, auto, home equity loans, credit card debt)	$ _____
Insurance (health, auto, homeowner, life, long-term care)	$ _____
Gifts, charitable contributions	$ _____
Investments	$ _____

	Total Monthly Expenses	$ _____
(multiply by 12)	Total Yearly Expenses	$ _____
(multiply by .90)	**TOTAL YEARLY RETIREMENT EXPENSES**	$ _____

Cash Flow Worksheet

Date: _____

INCOME	LAST YEAR	IN RETIREMENT
Wages or salary	$_____	$_____
Additional household wages or salary	$_____	$_____
Dividends and interest	$_____	$_____
Child support/alimony	$_____	$_____
Annuities, pensions, Social Security	$_____	$_____
Rents, royalties, fees	$_____	$_____
Other_____	$_____	$_____
TOTAL INCOME	$_____	$_____

TAXES		
Income taxes	$_____	$_____
Social Security contributions	$_____	$_____
Property taxes	$_____	$_____
Other_____	$_____	$_____
TOTAL TAXES	$_____	$_____

LIVING EXPENSES		
Rent or mortgage payments	$_____	$_____
Food	$_____	$_____
Clothing	$_____	$_____
Utilities	$_____	$_____
Meals out	$_____	$_____
Furniture and other durable goods	$_____	$_____
Recreation, entertainment, vacations	$_____	$_____
Gasoline	$_____	$_____
Car payments	$_____	$_____
Financial and legal services	$_____	$_____
Doctor, drugs, medical expenses	$_____	$_____
Interest	$_____	$_____
Household maintenance	$_____	$_____
Car repairs	$_____	$_____
Tuition/day care	$_____	$_____
Health care, life and disability insurance premiums	$_____	$_____
Grooming (i.e., laundry, cleaning)	$_____	$_____
Medications	$_____	$_____
Auto insurance premiums	$_____	$_____
Health insurance premiums	$_____	$_____
Other (i.e., gifts)	$_____	$_____
TOTAL ANNUAL LIVING EXPENSES	$_____	$_____

FUNDS AVAILABLE FOR SAVINGS AND INVESTMENTS (total income minus taxes & living expenses)	$_____	$_____

Net Worth Worksheet

Property Assets *

Residence	$_____
Vacation home	$_____
Furnishings	$_____
Jewelry/Art	$_____
Automobiles	$_____
Other	$_____

Equity Assets *

Real estate	$_____
Stocks	$_____
Mutual funds	$_____
Variable annuity	$_____
Business equity	$_____
Other	$_____

Cash Reserve Assets *

Checking account	$_____
Savings account	$_____
Credit union	$_____
CDs	$_____
Other	$_____

Fixed Assets *

Government bonds	$_____
Municipal bonds	$_____
Corporate bonds	$_____
Fixed annuities	$_____
Other	$_____
TOTAL ASSETS	$_____

Liabilities **

Home mortgage	$_____
Other mortgage	$_____
Bank loans	$_____
Auto loans	$_____
Personal loans	$_____
Credit card debt	$_____
Other	$_____
TOTAL LIABILITIES	$_____
TOTAL ASSETS (minus)	$_____
TOTAL LIABILITIES (equal)	– $_____
YOUR NET WORTH *** = $_____

This is your personal financial overview. You may be surprised at your net worth, especially if your home has appreciated significantly in value or if you have significant loans or credit card debt. Your cash flow and your net worth will provide the starting point for your financial future. By managing your cash flow, you can build your net worth and turn your dreams into realities.

---

*For calculation of your assets, use current value, not the original purchase price.

**Amounts due (not monthly installments but total balances) in accounts with credit card and gasoline companies, department stores and other retailers and to anyone else to whom you owe money. This is an important total to know and to review periodically; many who run into credit problems do so because they have lost track of how much they owe overall—It's too easy to charge.

***To compute your net worth, total your liabilities and deduct this amount from your total assets (if the amount is larger, you're facing trouble). The result is your net worth. After you've done this one, subsequent surveys will be easier; you will have basic figures that will only need reviewing and adjusting. A 20% increase in net worth annually is considered ideal—but don't really expect such a gain until later years.

> "Retirement can be a great joy if you can figure out how to spend time without spending money."
>
> —*Unknown*

Social Security

Social Security is an important financial component of your retirement planning. Some 63 million benefit payments go out each month. Social Security is essentially a family program that offers these major benefits:

- Disability benefits
- Survivor benefits
- Retirement benefits
- Medicare benefits

Benefits can also be paid to dependents of retired, disabled or deceased workers (refer to the dependent benefits chart, page 32). Each of the major benefits will be discussed in more detail later. Social Security acts as a kind of insurance at important junctures in your family's life: retirement, disability and death.

Becoming Insured

For any benefits to be paid, the worker must have worked long enough and sometimes recently enough to qualify. Work performed under Social Security earns quarters of coverage (or credits). Four credits can be earned in a calendar year. Before 1978, a worker had to actually earn $50 or more during a calendar quarter to earn a credit. Beginning in 1978, yearly credits are determined by dividing the total covered earnings by a yearly increment. These increments increase every year. In 2019, one credit is earned for each $1,360; therefore, $5,440 will earn the four-credit maximum.

The number of credits needed depends on the type of benefit involved. As a rule of thumb, one credit is needed for each year that elapses after age 21 up to the year of age 62, death or disability. It does not matter when the credits are earned. Disability benefits require the worker not only to be fully insured but also to have recent work. Some survivor benefits can be paid if the worker is not fully insured but has earned credits in six of the thirteen calendar quarters prior to death. By doing so, the worker is considered to be currently insured. This is especially helpful when young workers die, leaving dependent children and widows/ers or former widows/ers caring for those children.

Some people think that their Social Security benefits will be based on the number of credits they have. This is not true. The dollar amount of any benefits paid has nothing to do with the number of credits you have. You either qualify or do not qualify for benefits based on credits. The calculation of the benefit amount will be discussed later.

If Retirement Is Far Away

The Social Security Administration has been keeping records of your earnings throughout your working life. Are those records accurate and up to date? Imagine filing for your benefits and finding yourself shortchanged or delayed because of errors made years ago.

Year of Birth	Full Retirement Age (FRA)**
1941	65 and 8 months
1942	65 and 10 months
1943-54	66
1955	66 and 2 months
1956	66 and 4 months
1957	66 and 6 months
1958	66 and 8 months
1959	66 and 10 months
1960 and later	67

* This chart does not apply to survivor benefits.
** If you take monthly benefits before FRA, your benefits are reduced. Medicare is still available at age 65, regardless of FRA.

Check Your Records: To get your estimate, go to ssa.gov/benefits/retirement/estimator.html, call 800-772-1213 or set up your free, personal account at ssa.gov/myaccount. Social Security mails annual benefit statements to workers age 60 and over who aren't receiving Social Security benefits and haven't set up an account. At least every three years, request a statement of your earnings from Social Security. Review your statement carefully, and report any errors *immediately* to the Social Security office nearest you. You can do this by telephone. Note the date, time and name of the person you spoke with in your own records.

Check for Overpayments: You may also find an employer did not stop collecting Social Security taxes after reaching the maximum taxable amount in a given year or you worked for more than one employer and your total wages exceeded the maximum. In this event, you can receive a refund or a credit against your federal income tax. Request it on your income tax return.

Retirement Benefits

Full retirement age (FRA) is the age at which you could be entitled to a full unreduced retirement benefit or spousal benefit. (See chart on this page.) Very few people find their Social Security checks sufficient to cover their expenses. We suggest you find out what you can expect from Social Security and how it will fit into your retirement plans. Your Social Security retirement benefits will be based on your lifetime earnings. Many people think that only the last five years are used to calculate benefits. Nothing could be further from the truth. Everyone born in 1929 and later will have 35 years of earnings averaged together to determine their benefit computation.

For an explanation of how retirement benefits are figured, ask Social Security for the fact sheet *Your Retirement Benefit: How It's Figured,* or visit www.ssa.gov/pubs/EN-05-10070.pdf.

Early vs. Late Retirement

As you look ahead to retirement, you may be thinking "The earlier, the better." But if Social Security is going to be your only source of income, "the later, the better" applies.

Early retirement decreases your retirement benefits. If you take your benefits before full retirement age (FRA), they are permanently reduced. The amount of the reduction depends on the number of months you elect benefits prior to full retirement age. **SPECIAL NOTE:** Even if you file for reduced benefits, at FRA you will be given credit for any months you did not receive a full check because of work. This is commonly referred to by Social Security as an automatic adjustment of your reduction factor.

If you decide to retire before FRA, or you have very low earnings, you should consider filing early. For a more detailed explanation of the best time to contact Social Security to avoid possible loss of benefits, refer to the section entitled "When to Contact" (page 34).

If you decline benefits at FRA or later, your benefit is increased for each month after FRA (delayed retirement credits). The percentage of these delayed credits increases over time and will reach 8%.

At FRA, you may have other options:

- File and Restrict: You can file a Social Security application and restrict that application to receive benefits from the work record of your current or prior spouse. This option, called the deemed filing rule, might allow you to receive monthly benefits while preserving your ability to earn delayed retirement credits (DRC) on your own work record. Your current spouse must have established entitlement to retirement or disability Social Security monthly benefits. Note: This option will expire January 1, 2020. If you are filing on the divorced spouse's work record, that spouse must be entitled to retirement or disability, file and suspend his or her benefits before April 30, 2016 or be eligible for retirement, i.e., have enough work credits and be at least age 62. You must also have been divorced for at least two years.

Keep in mind these two options are only available at FRA.

As a quick check on how much you can look forward to at FRA, consider what percentage of your income will be replaced by your retirement benefits. If your lifetime earnings were average, you can expect to receive a benefit of about $17,532 a year. An eligible couple with average earnings receives about $29,376 a year (both worker and spouse at full retirement age).

If you have always paid the maximum in Social Security deductions, you can count on a benefit of about 26% of that amount. In 2019, the maximum earnings subject to Social Security taxes are $132,900, generating $34,332 a year in retirement benefits. As long as you work you will pay FICA taxes.

Spouses

Both spouses are eligible to receive Social Security benefits, even if only one has earned enough credits. The worker who qualifies will receive at retirement his or her own benefits. The nonqualified spouse (the spouse who has not worked enough to qualify) will receive a benefit equal to a percentage of the worker's benefit. Usually the nonqualified spouse must be age 62 to receive this spousal benefit.

If both spouses qualify on their own for Social Security, both will receive their own benefits. In those instances where one spouse's FRA benefit is less than half of the other's FRA amount, the lesser-paid spouse will usually receive his or her own benefit *plus* a spousal benefit.

The spousal benefit provisions in no way reduce the worker's benefits. Similarly, spousal benefits payable to the current spouse are not affected by any benefits being paid to a former spouse.

Important to note is that though a spouse may be eligible for benefits at age 62 *without* having worked, the same is not true for disability benefits. You must have worked *and* meet certain other conditions to receive disability benefits. There are no disabled spouse benefits.

Social Security Tables

Remember, the maximum amount of earnings covered by Social Security was lower in past years than it is now. Those years of lower limits must be counted in with the higher ones of recent years to figure your average earnings and the amount of your monthly retirement benefit payment.

Estimate Monthly and First-Year Social Security Income Payable in 2019 to a Person Attaining Full Retirement Age (FRA)

(1) Salary in Year Before Retirement	(2) Monthly	(3) First Year Social Security Income	(4) Approximate Replacement Ratio
$30,000	$1,014	$12,168	41%
$40,000	$1,224	$14,688	37%
$50,000	$1,307	$15,684	34%
$60,000	$1,376	$16,512	28%
$90,000	$2,053	$24,632	27%
$120,000	$2,334	$28,008	23%
$132,900	$2,438	$29,256	22%

Notes to chart: Because $128,400 was the maximum taxable 2018 Social Security wage base, Social Security will, of course, replace an increasingly smaller portion of earnings that exceed it.

Maximum benefits for a worker attaining FRA in 2019 is $2,861 per month. Replacement rate numbers are only tentative until prior year average wages are determined.

These figures assume you have worked regularly and received yearly wage increases.

Note: For a couple with average earnings, the Social Security benefit is about $29,376 a year (both worker and spouse at full retirement age).

The Social Security tables are based on assumptions for people attaining FRA in 2019 who earned the salaries shown in 2018, assuming they had worked steadily for equivalent wages since age 22.

Except for persons who have always paid the maximum, the amount payable in any particular case could vary greatly from those illustrated.

In fact, persons spending much of their careers either in *noncovered* employment or *outside* the workforce altogether will likely receive less payment.

AUTOMATIC SOCIAL SECURITY COST-OF-LIVING ADJUSTMENTS

Once you are on the Social Security rolls, your benefit payments will increase automatically to keep pace with increases in the cost of living.

In addition, additional earnings after initial entitlement can be considered in a recalculation of your rate.

The tables also assume that the worker does not qualify for a noncovered pension.

Anyone who does qualify for a pension based on work that was not covered for Social Security taxes may not have the same computation method. Social Security can provide a fact sheet titled *Windfall Elimination Provision* that explains this in detail. In addition, a noncovered pension can affect benefits from your spouse's record. Review the fact sheet *Government Pension Offset*.

Survivor Benefits

Survivor benefits to dependent children and young widows/ers can be paid, based on fully or currently insured status. The amount of benefits payable to any survivor is determined by the covered earnings of the deceased worker.

A rate is calculated as if the worker was age 62 in the year of death, and a primary insurance amount (PIA) is established. Each dependent is entitled to a percentage of the PIA; however, there is a maximum amount payable. (Refer to the chart on page 32 for more specific information.)

A one-time death payment of $255 is payable to either a widow/er entitled to benefits or a widow/er not entitled to monthly benefits or to children entitled to benefits.

Benefits due to divorced spouses are not considered in the family maximum. In other words, the divorced spouse takes nothing away from the current spouse or widow and vice versa.

Widows and Widowers

Today, in many families, both spouses have worked and paid Social Security. Most qualify for retirement as early as age 62. Some may have been widowed and received Social Security benefits prior to age 62 as a widow/er benefit. This person at reaching the age of 62 should check with Social Security and find out the dollar amount of a retirement payment they could receive if they filed for benefits based on their own work record. If the widow/er qualified for a higher rate, he or she could switch to his or her own record. For widows/ers born prior to January 2, 1940, full retirement age for survivor benefits is still age 65. For those born after January 1, 1945, FRA for unreduced survivor benefits is age 65 and 10 months. For those born between January 2, 1945 and January 1, 1946, FRA for unreduced survivor benefits is age 66.

OTHER RESOURCES

Social Security Administration provides pamphlets. Call toll-free 1-800-772-1213 to request copies, or visit www.ssa.gov/pubs.

- Windfall Elimination Provision
- If You Are a Farm Worker
- Government Pension Offset
- How Workers' Compensation and Other Disability Payments May Affect Your Benefits
- Household Workers
- How Work Affects Your Benefits
- Your Retirement Benefit: How It Is Figured
- Military Service and Social Security
- If You Are Self-Employed
- What You Need to Know: Reviewing Your Disability
- Your Right to Representation
- Special Payments After Retirement
- The Appeals Process
- When You Retire From Your Own Business: What You Need to Know

3 WAYS TO ENSURE A SOUND FINANCIAL RETIREMENT

Social Security Benefits for Dependents

Dependent Is Age	And	Then These Benefits May Be Payable	At the Following Percent of PIA***
0–19	A child of a deceased or entitled worker*	Minor child or student benefits	50% (worker alive) 75% (worker deceased)
18 and older	disabled before age 22 and parent is either deceased or entitled	disabled adult child benefits	50% (worker alive) 75% (worker deceased)
Up to FRA**	A young widow/er or divorced widow/er with child in care under age 16	Mother/father benefits	75%
50–60	A disabled widow/er or a surviving divorced widow/er	Disabled widow/er benefits	71.5%
60+	A widow/er, surviving divorced spouse	Widow/ers benefit	Varies from 71.5% to 100%, depending on age at entitlement
62+	1. Currently married to entitled worker	Spouse benefits	Varies from 22.8% to 50%, depending on age at entitlement
	2. Divorced after 10 years of marriage to entitled worker	Divorced spouse benefits	
	3. Divorced after 10 years of marriage to an age 62 worker not entitled but insured	Independently entitled divorced spouse benefits	
	4. Surviving parent(s)		Parent benefits 82.5%, if one 75% each, if two

There is a family maximum of benefits that can be paid on a worker's record. To keep within the family maximum, benefits for dependents may have to be adjusted.
*See Chapter 15 for information for grandchildren. **Full retirement age ***Primary insurance amount

Before you decide to switch, we recommend that you find out what the dollar amount of your own retirement benefits would be at 62, at FRA, and at age 70. Most widows/ers are told the rates for age 62 and FRA; however, most Social Security employees fail to tell you what the rate would be if you wait until age 70. At age 70, delayed retirement credits can be added to your own basic retirement benefit and will significantly increase the total retirement check.

There have been many widows/ers who were told that there was no need to file a claim on their own work because the widows/ers rate was higher. They were not advised that if they waited until age 70 to file on their own work record, their own retirement check amount would exceed the widow/er rate. There are also many widows who are eligible on the records of more than one prior spouse. Such widows need to examine their choices carefully.

Disability Benefits

The risk of disability hangs over all of us. A loss of earnings due to severe injury or illness can affect a family more than retirement or death.

Social Security provides basic protection against disability for most Americans and their families. Currently, about 8 million adults receive disability benefit payments. There is a five-month waiting period before disability payments can begin. This period begins with the first full month of disability and ends five months later. *No payment is made for that period.*

As mentioned earlier, under Social Security a disabled worker must be fully insured and have recent work in order to be qualified. During the ten-year period just before becoming disabled, the worker must have five years of credits (20). **Workers becoming disabled prior to age 31 need fewer credits.** Workers who are statutorily blind must only be fully insured.

It is very important for a worker to understand the "recent work" requirement, particularly persons opting for "early out" retirements with their company. If you plan on retiring prior to age 56, you should consider working at another job and acquiring four credits per year *through the year* you attain age 56. By doing so, you will continue to have enough recent work to qualify you for disability until you reach age 62.

Dependents of disabled workers can also receive benefits within the family maximum payable.

Medicare Benefits

Medicare is a national health insurance program for people who are age 65, have been receiving Social Security disability benefits for 24 months,

SOCIAL SECURITY PAYMENT DATES

New beneficiaries will have their benefits directly deposited based on day of birth:

1-10	2nd Wednesday of the month
11-20	3rd Wednesday of the month
21-31	4th Wednesday of the month

have end-stage renal disease, or become disabled due to ALS or asbestos-related lung disease from Libby, Montana. It is administered by the Social Security Administration. The Department of Health and Human Services is responsible for processing reimbursements for covered medical services.

Whether or not you apply for Social Security at age 65, you should apply at least three months in advance of your 65th birthday to be covered by Medicare. (See Chapter 7.)

Work and Social Security

With the exception of a disabled worker or an adult disabled child, *all* Social Security beneficiaries are subject to an earnings test up until the month they attain FRA (see chart on page 28). There is a yearly limit on the amount of earnings you can have before withholding some of your benefits. These limits increase every year.

If you are less than FRA throughout 2019, the earnings limit is $17,640. For persons attaining FRA in 2019, the limit is $46,920; however, only earnings up to the month of FRA are counted. There is no limit once you reach FRA. Earnings during the month you become FRA and thereafter do not count toward the annual limit. Earnings include only income from work or from self-employment. Investment income (dividends, real estate, rentals, and return on capital) is *not* counted as earnings. Neither are pensions.

If you earn more than the yearly limit, you will lose some of your Social Security benefits. One dollar is withheld for every two dollars above the limit for all persons younger than FRA throughout the year. One dollar in benefits will be deducted for each three dollars you earn above the annual limit

EARNINGS LIMIT IN YEAR OF ATTAINMENT OF FRA

2019	$46,920

Annual exempt amount indexed to growth in wages.

for persons attaining FRA during the year. This "one for three" rule is significant. Many people could receive some Social Security benefits for months before FRA even while working full-time.

There is a special rule that can apply to your initial year of retirement. It is called the "grace year" rule, meaning that workers are allowed a monthly earning limit for each month in that year. The monthly limit is simply the annual limit divided by twelve. This special rule usually applies only for one year but helps those persons who have high earnings in the months prior to retirement.

Ask Social Security for the fact sheet *How Work Affects Your Social Security Benefits*.

When to Contact

Survivors of deceased workers should contact Social Security as soon as possible after the death of the worker. Disabled workers should contact Social Security as soon as their physician advises that their medical condition is expected to last at least twelve months.

We recommend that all other persons should:

■ Contact Social Security three months prior to age 62 if you have retired or are planning to retire at age 62.

SOCIAL SECURITY: THEN AND NOW

When the Social Security Act was passed, the average American died at 63. Most people wouldn't live to collect Social Security, and those who did wouldn't collect it for long.

Today, the average American will live to about 78, actually 76 for men and 81 for women.

When Social Security was launched in 1937, more than 40 contributors supported each recipient. Until 1949, the maximum contribution was $30 per year. A lot has changed since then. Longevity has increased. Social Security has expanded to include more benefits and more recipients.

OR

■ Contact Social Security every January (even if working full-time). Provide them with an estimate of your current year earnings and ask them to determine the dollar amount of any benefits you might be eligible for if you filed a formal claim. Remember to tell Social Security if there are any dependents who will also be eligible for benefits on your record. In many cases a worker is better off to file for benefits effective with January of the year they become FRA rather than effective with the month they become FRA.

AND

■ Regardless of when you retire, be sure to contact Social Security three months prior to age 65 for Medicare benefits. As mentioned earlier, although FRA has increased, Medicare is still effective as of age 65.

Benefits May Be Taxable

Up to 85% of your benefits may be subject to the federal income tax for any year in which your adjusted gross income plus non-taxable interest income and one-half of your Social Security benefits exceed a base amount of $25,000 for an individual, $32,000 for a couple, and zero for a couple filing separately. If you would like to have income taxes withheld from your check, contact Social Security.

Supplemental Security Income

People in financial need who are 65 or older or people of any age who are blind or disabled may be eligible for a monthly cash payment from the federal government. These payments are called supplemental security income (SSI).

People may be eligible for payments if they have little or no regular cash income and don't own much in the way of assets that can be turned into cash. The Social Security Administration operates the program, but SSI is not the same as Social Security. Social Security funds are not used to make SSI payments. Applications for SSI are made at the Social Security office. In most states, Medicaid is provided for anyone eligible for SSI.

of death. "Taxable estate" is the gross estate less liabilities. Don't assume that your spouse will automatically receive your property. Even if you have all your property jointly owned, the absence of a will may cause your spouse to wait several months before gaining possession of the property.

Owning Property

Check with your attorney: which of the four types of property ownership best suits your needs?

- **Joint Tenancy With Right of Survivorship:** Two or more people hold property jointly and one person dies—the other or others receive the dead person's interest.

- **Tenancy by the Entirety:** Limited to spouses. Both spouses have to agree as to disposal of the property.

- **Tenancy in Common:** When two or more people hold shares in property and one dies, his or her shares pass to that person's heirs.

- **Community Property:** Nine states have laws holding that all property acquired during marriage is owned by each spouse equally.

Why Make a Will?

A will is a written instrument executed with the formalities prescribed by law, whereby a person directs the disposition of his or her property after death.

Not having a will can result in disaster for your loved ones. Your assets will be divided according to state law and not your wishes. Without a will, you will leave your family dangerously vulnerable and the court will decide who will raise your children. Your will should name a guardian and a trustee to manage your estate on their behalf.

If you make a will, your property will go to the person(s) named and in the amounts you specify. If you fail to make a will, the law arbitrarily distributes your property according to prevailing regulations.

> "In this world nothing can be said to be certain, except death and taxes."
>
> —*Benjamin Franklin*

Planning Your Estate

What will happen in the event of your death?

Will your estate be turned over to your family without loss? Carelessness in making plans for your estate increases the chances that it may be disposed of in ways you would not approve of.

Before skipping to the next chapter, thinking that you don't have an estate and that everything will be left to your spouse, let's define what is an estate. You may not have much to leave when you die, but the U.S. government may have a less modest opinion of what you are leaving. The federal estate tax rate is 40% for those estates worth more than $11.18 million. Check, as there may be changes made to these federal taxes. Consult with an estate attorney to see how these taxes will affect your estate.

An estate consists of life insurance, accounts in banks and credit unions, Social Security, stocks, pension, real estate, business and professional interests, investments, etc.

For the purpose of taxation, the "gross estate" is composed of all assets and property owned at the time of death and gifts made in contemplation

When You Don't Have a Will...

Making a will may save money. Without a will: Your heirs will not be able to sell, distribute or handle property without the expense of asking a court for authority; your estate or inheritance taxes may be higher than they need legally be; the person who administers your estate will have to post a bond, the premium for which must be taken from the estate; your property may be dealt with; your business may be operated or concluded; and your real estate may be sold with losses.

If you make a will, you can name the person you wish to handle your estate. The administrator or executor can liquidate your assets, pay your taxes and debts and disburse the property to your heirs. Where no will exists, the matter of who will administer the estate can be the occasion for painful disputes and needless expense.

When preparing your will, also have a power of attorney and health care proxy prepared. This gives someone you trust authority to make financial and medical decisions if you are incapacitated.

Disposition of Estates

You can use a will to make outright disposition of your assets. You can also make outright gifts of parcels of your estate during your lifetime. You can gift up to $15,000 a year (or $30,000 per couple) without incurring a gift tax. You can create a trust by transferring your estate, or part of it, to a trustee. You may live off the income it provides during your lifetime, with the principal being disposed of later. You can also set up a testamentary trust that assures income for your spouse or dependents. This type of arrangement protects them against their own inexperience in the management of the estate. If you receive an inheritance, protect your newfound wealth. Visit a financial planner to make a plan. Don't make hasty decisions.

Keeping Wills Up to Date

Wills should be reviewed every 3-5 years. Circumstances may have changed such that particulars referred to in the will no longer exist or things exist that the original will did not cover.

The following changes should cause you to look *again* at the condition of your will:

- Change of mind about beneficiaries.
- Executor dies.
- Change in family situation.
- Change in financial situation.
- Change in the nature of assets.
- Change in the needs of the beneficiaries.
- Change of residence, state or country.

Consider Trusts

Trusts may be an ideal method to handle some of your assets. A trust can be a valuable estate planning tool because it will bypass probate. With a trust, you can name yourself trustee and also name a successor trustee or have a fiduciary trustee manage it according to a written agreement.

Trusts may be living or testamentary, revocable or irrevocable. Example: You wish to transfer $20,000 to a trust for your grandchildren's education while you're alive—a living trust. If the trust was created by your will, it's testamentary.

A revocable trust can be canceled by the person who establishes it. In a revocable trust, assets remain accessible to you during your lifetime, and it designates to whom the remaining assets will be passed to. An irrevocable trust cannot be terminated. Choose carefully.

Trusts have advantages under certain conditions. They could save money and time. Consult your attorney and accountant.

Power of Attorney

Power of attorney allows someone to act as your agent while you are alive. Do not give away any more control than you absolutely have to. You can revoke your power of attorney at any time as long as you are mentally capable. This power can be very specific or broad and can include details such as handling your checking account, filing taxes or selling/buying a house. A general power of attorney will cover all your financial and personal decisions, while a limited power of attorney allows the agent to handle only specific matters, usually when you are unavailable or unable to do so. You should designate the scope of the responsibilities and/or the time period during which your agent can act for you. If you become incapacitated, these powers will cease and you will need a durable power of attorney.

Documents Needed

A **durable power of attorney** names someone, typically a spouse, to make financial decisions for you when you are medically disabled.

A **living will** is not part of your will. It states your wishes to health care providers as to what artificial life-sustaining procedures you want in the event of a terminal illness and you are unable to make decisions.

A **durable power of attorney for health care** should be prepared at the same time as your living will. It is also known as a health care proxy or durable medical power of attorney. It makes clear your wishes about your future medical care. It tells doctors and hospital employees whether you want to be kept alive if you're in a coma or suffering a terminal illness beyond all reasonable hope of recovery. It names someone you trust to carry out your wishes. You should name a second person in the event the first is not available. It is important to communicate with your agent in advance what

you desire and have them agree to fulfill your wishes. You can specify what should be done after consultation with family members and doctors—check with an attorney or your local office of aging. All family members over the age of 18 should have this.

A Legal Checklist

- Review your finances, assets and debts with your spouse and family.

- Prepare a letter of instruction, which should include your funeral arrangements, where to find your documents and how to handle your personal property.

- Prepare a will with an estate lawyer, which will allow you to choose who will receive your assets, oversee your estate and name a guardian to look after your children.

- Review current beneficiary designations that are not covered in your will, such as your IRA, insurance policies, annuities and company benefit plans.

- Consider creating a living trust.

- Prepare advance directives such as a power of attorney and a durable power of attorney for health care.

- Set up a file in your home with your important papers. Tell a trusted person where they are.

Will Fact Sheet

Name: _____ Date this form completed: _____

Telephone number at home: _____ At work: _____

Street address: _____

City: _____ County: _____ State: _____ ZIP code: _____

	Yourself	Your Spouse
Name:		
Social Security Number:		
Occupation:		
Date and place of birth:		
Driver's license number:		
Military service:		
Date/place of marriage:		
Date of divorce:		
Death of spouse:		

Children

Name (also of spouse): _____ Date and place of birth: _____

Telephone number at home: _____ At work: _____

Street address: _____

City: _____ County: _____ State: _____ ZIP code: _____

Name (also of spouse): _____ Date and place of birth: _____

Telephone number at home: _____ At work: _____

Street address: _____

City: _____ County: _____ State: _____ ZIP code: _____

Name (also of spouse): _____ Date and place of birth: _____

Telephone number at home: _____ At work: _____

Street address: _____

City: _____ County: _____ State: _____ ZIP code: _____

Benefit Plans

Pension plan: _____ Value (if known): $ _____

Thrift plan: _____ Value (if known): $ _____

Profit-sharing plan: _____ Value (if known): $ _____

Other: _____ Value (if known): $ _____

Other: _____ Value (if known): $ _____

Other: _____ Value (if known): $ _____

Other: _____ Value (if known): $ _____

Other: _____ Value (if known): $ _____

Health Insurance

Company: _____ Policy number: _____

Street address: _____ Agent: _____

City/State/ZIP code: _____ Beneficiaries _____

Telephone: _____ Location of policy: _____

Company: _____ Policy number: _____

Street address: _____ Agent: _____

City/State/ZIP code: _____ Beneficiaries _____

Telephone: _____ Location of policy: _____

Home and Auto Insurance

Company: _____ Policy number: _____

Street address: _____ Agent: _____

City/State/ZIP code: _____ Type of Coverage _____

Telephone: _____ Location of policy: _____

Company: _____ Policy number: _____

Street address: _____ Agent: _____

City/State/ZIP code: _____ Type of Coverage _____

Telephone: _____ Location of policy: _____

Assets Inventory

	Current Value	Original Cost	Ownership	Location
Home:				
Business:				
Savings account:				
Checking account:				
Pension plans:				
Household furniture:				
Collections:				
Bonds:				
Trust funds:				
Stocks:				
Other:				

Have a list of your email address, PINs and passwords so your family can access your records in case of emergency.

Liability Inventory

Loans:	Amount: $
Debts:	Amount: $
Mortgages:	Amount: $
Other:	Amount: $

Life Insurance

Company/agent:	Face amount of policy:
Type of policy:	Cash surrender value:
Policy number:	Accidental death provision:
Telephone:	Beneficiaries:
Company/agent:	Face amount of policy:
Type of policy:	Cash surrender value:
Policy number:	Accidental death provision:
Telephone:	Beneficiaries:

Location of Records, Licenses, etc.

Birth:	Deed:
Marriage:	Mortgage:
Adoption:	Title policy insurance:
Citizenship:	Title abstract:
Pre/postnuptial:	Surveys:
Divorce:	Insurance policies:
Discharge papers:	Tax receipts:
Building costs:	Leases:

Safe Deposit Box

Institution where located:	Box number:
Street address:	Who has access:
City, state, ZIP code:	Location of key:
Contents:	

A list of how you would like your personal effects distributed (jewelry, art, etc.) and your burial instructions should be placed in a safe place but *not* in your safe deposit box.

People Who Know About My Affairs

Attorney:	Telephone number:
Power of attorney:	Telephone number:
Accountant:	Telephone number:
Broker:	Telephone number:
Doctor:	Telephone number:
Banker:	Telephone number:
Clergy/rabbi:	Telephone number:
Employer/union rep:	Telephone number:
Insurance agent:	Telephone number:
Executor of estate:	Telephone number:

"Cloud nine gets all the publicity, but cloud eight actually is cheaper, less crowded and has a better view."
—*George Carlin*

Hanging on to Your Money

Hanging on to your retirement money is often a difficult task, but by keeping your eyes wide open, you can avoid the common pitfalls that threaten to deplete your pocketbook.

The Purchaser

Studies show that the typical consumer's buying habits needlessly strain their budget.

- Most grocery shoppers never use a list and shop in only one grocery store.
- Customers who charge their purchases buy three times as much as those who pay cash.
- Many buy nonessential items on credit for which they should pay with cash.
- Many people do not know how to budget their paycheck to last throughout the month.

It is estimated that as much as 20% of the average grocery bill could be saved if some simple rules were followed. The average family spends about 29% of its budget on food. If your income is $2,000 a month, your food budget could be $580. A savings of 20% would provide the same amount of food for $464.

Saving at the Market

Consider the following:

- Always plan your food shopping. Make and use a list, and avoid impulse buying.
- *Never* shop while hungry.
- Shop only once or twice a week.
- Avoid paying for packaging.
- Consider buying the local store's brand.
- Avoid diet foods, if possible. Buy regular foods, and eat less. (However, if you are on a special diet prescribed by your doctor, you should stay with what is recommended.)
- Learn to compare cost per unit/price. Buying the larger size may not save you money.
- Learn to substitute fish, poultry or smaller quantities of meat for meals that rely heavily on meat.

Credit Bureaus

For every credit offer you receive, a corresponding inquiry has been made into your credit report.

Under the Fair Credit Reporting Act, credit bureaus are required to set up toll-free numbers so that consumers can call to opt out of preapproved credit offers. A phone call to one of the following services will close your credit file for two years:

- Equifax 800-685-1111
  www.equifax.com
- Experian 888-397-3742
  www.experian.com
- Trans Union 800-916-8800
  www.transunion.com

To help protect your identity, you can freeze your credit report by mailing a certified letter to each of the 3 bureaus. The cost varies by state. To request your free annual credit report, check www.annualcreditreport.com or call 877-322-8228. This report does not include your credit score, which can be ordered for a fee. Don't use freecreditreport.com because it could sign you to a fee-based service.

Credit Cards: Easy to Abuse

Credit cards are easy to get—Be careful. Pay cash and stay out of trouble. The thinking that goes into a cash transaction should go into a credit card transaction. Pay your credit card in full each month. Call your credit card issuer if you are having problems making payments; they may be able to help make the payments easier.

KEEP IN MIND: When you charge a purchase on a credit card and do not pay for it in full when the bill comes in, interest charges begin.

Drawback to Debit Cards

Some merchants add a fee similar to an ATM fee. For some purchases, the merchant places a hold on your account much greater than you have charged. This may cause you trouble.

You also have less leverage in disputes with merchants when you use a debit card. Under federal law, a credit card offers strong protection, letting you refuse to pay until the dispute is settled. Debit cards offer no such protection.

You'll have even less protection against loss or theft. Federal law limits your maximum liability on your credit card to $50, provided you notify the card company within 60 days. A debit card is not covered by federal law. You must report the loss or theft within two business days (some banks allow more time) to limit your loss to $50; after two days, it is raised to $500. After 60 days, there is no cap. Every penny in your account and in any linked credit line is at risk.

Insurance

Picking insurance policies can be confusing. Policies differ. What sounds similar may have features that change the premium.

Even two identical policies can vary considerably in cost from one insurer to another. Before you purchase, make sure you are dealing with a reputable company and compare its premium with those of competitors. To help you evaluate the premium expenses, check www.AccuQuote.com.

Telemarketing

Chances are you've been called by telemarketers, often at inconvenient times, and with a sales pitch for products and contests that don't interest you. Some may be fraudulent. Know your telemarketing rights. The Federal Trade Commission (FTC) created the National Do Not Call Registry. To register, call 888-382-1222 (you must call from the number you wish to register) or visit www .donotcall.gov. Most telemarketers cannot call your telephone number if it is in the National Do Not Call Registry. Registration is free.

Stop the Scams

People over 60 account for about 30% of fraud victims, according to Consumer Action. Don't be pressured into signing a contract.

- Resist high-pressure sales tactics. Legitimate businesses respect that you're not interested.
- If you don't want the seller to call you back, say so; if they call back, hang up. They're breaking the law.
- Take your time. Ask for written information about the subject of the call.
- Your financial investments may have consequences. Before you respond to a phone

CREDIT CARD DEBT

By paying more than the minimum monthly payment, you can reduce the overall interest charged to you. If you owe $1,000 on a credit card that charges 14.45%, paying off just an extra $10 to $30 a month shortens the payoff period **and saves you interest and money.**

Monthly Payment	Total Interest	Time to Pay Off
$20 (minimum)	$540	77 months
$30	$290	43 months
$50	$200	24 months

Paying off your credit card debt is the best investment you can make.

solicitation, talk to a friend, family member or financial advisor.

- Don't pay for prizes. Free is free!
- Don't send cash, check or money order by courier, overnight delivery or wire to anyone who insists on immediate payment.
- Never give your credit card, bank account, or Social Security number to a telemarketer.
- Suspect a scam? Call your state attorney general.

Health Insurance Scams

Bogus health care plans are one of the biggest consumer insurance frauds. To avoid being scammed, get the salesperson's name, telephone number, address and business license, call your state's insurance dept. and ask if the company or agent is licensed to do business in the state and if any action has been taken against them. The local Better Business Bureaus also collect complaint information. Brokers must be registered with the Financial Industry Regulatory Authority. The NASAA Senior Investor Resource Center at http://serveourseniors.org provides tips on preventing fraud.

No one should be pressured into making a decision on the spot. Never provide bank account or credit card information to get locked-in premiums. There is no "ObamaCare" plan being marketed or sold by the federal government.

Identity Theft

More than 12 million people have been victims of identity theft. Many times your first knowledge of the theft is when you receive notification from a collection agency or charges appear on your credit card. Steps you can take to prevent identity theft:

- Identity theft of children is 51 times higher than of adults. Contact credit agencies, file a child-identity inquiry and order a credit freeze.
- Never leave your purse or wallet in your car.
- Only carry credit cards that you need, and carry no more than two at one time.
- Write *Ask for ID* instead of your signature on the back of your credit card.
- Reconcile your checking account regularly.
- Never carry your Social Security card or birth certificate.
- Carry your Medicare card only when visiting your doctor.
- Review your medical statements. Do not give your insurance information to someone who calls you, unless you know them.
- Do not keep ATM personal identification numbers (PIN) or passwords in your wallet.
- Carry your passport only when traveling.
- Keep a list or a copy, at home, of all your credit and bank accounts; include account numbers, expiration dates, and telephone numbers of the customer service departments.
- Put passwords on your credit cards, bank and phone accounts.
- Ask your credit card issuer to add an instant alert service on your account.
- Do not have your Social Security or driver's license number printed on your checks.
- Give your Social Security number only when necessary. Use other types of identification.
- Review your credit reports every year from a credit bureau. See page 42.

- Cut up or shred preapproved credit offers that you will not use. To stop receiving credit offers, call 888-5-OPTOUT or go to www.optoutprescreen.com.

- Never give personal information (credit card number, driver's license number, Social Security number, birth date, mother's maiden name) unless you know to whom you are speaking.

- Place outgoing mail containing personal information (i.e., bills) in a secure mailbox. Make sure your incoming mail is placed in a secure mailbox.

- Do not write account numbers on the outside of envelopes. Do not put your full credit card number on your check; just put the last 4 digits.

- Keep tax records, canceled checks and bills in a secure place, or shred them before throwing them away.

- If you are the victim of identity theft, file a police report to submit to creditors and others that may require proof of the crime. Call your financial institutions immediately.

- Change your password, and make it complicated. Update the virus and firewall protection on your computer frequently.

- Ordering on the Internet? Make sure it's a secure site.

- Don't give personal information on social networks.

- On a website, don't answer security questions honestly, such as birthplace, etc.

- When using public Wi-Fi, never assume it is secure. Do not pay bills or enter your name or passwords in public.

- Home aides and retirement home staff have access to records. Keep papers locked up.

- In an obituary, do not give birth date and month, only the year, and mail death certificate to all three credit bureaus. Have them mark it as deceased. Notify your State Dept. of Motor Vehicles.

- For more information, contact privacyrights.org or the National Consumers League's Fraud Center at www.fraud.org.

IDENTITY THEFT

If you have been a victim of identity theft, contact the Federal Trade Commission's Identity Theft Hotline at 877-IDTHEFT, or mail Identity Theft Clearinghouse, Federal Trade Commission, 600 Pennsylvania Avenue NW, Washington, DC 20580, or visit www.identitytheft.gov.

If you believe someone is using your Social Security number, call the Social Security Administration's Fraud Hotline at 800-269-0271.

Internet Fraud

Imposter scams account for 13% of consumer complaints to the Federal Trade Commission. Treat all information that you receive on the Internet as you would any unsolicited information. **Never** make an investment without getting all the facts. Get financial statements, verify claims and check with your financial planner, broker or attorney. If something looks too good to be true, be suspicious and take care. Be wary. Many websites mimic the look of a legitimate company; this is called phishing. If you have not requested information, **do not** open these emails. **Never** give your account or password information.

For more information, check with the U.S. Securities and Exchange Commission at www.sec.gov or 800-732-0330. To file a complaint, go to www.IC3.gov, the Internet Crime Complaint Center, and your state attorney general's office.

Home Equity Loans

With many financial institutions, equity loans are straightforward, with no hidden costs. Sadly, others don't maintain such standards.

Do not be pressured into signing a home equity loan. First, obtain advice. Discuss your financial status frankly with your bank or credit union. They may have helpful ideas or can refer you to sources for advice. You may not need the loan.

Rebates and Coupons

Rebates and coupons can save money, but they may not be for you. Some rebates and coupons are offered to introduce a new product, while others aim to sell a product that is overstocked. Decide if you really do need the item; then, comparison shop. If you do buy, you'll then have the problem of applying for the rebate. In most rebates, the bar code from the product's package must be mailed in with a proof of purchase within a certain time. Many people simply do not follow through.

Mutual Fund Expenses

There are differences in costs of mutual funds. The difference can translate into a lot of money over a period of time. Mutual fund loads (fees) range from $5^3/_4\%$ to as low as $^1/_2\%$. If we assume an average return of 8% and an average upfront load of 3%, the investor would have a return of 5% after fees, a considerable difference over the years.

Tax Returns

If you use a commercial tax firm to file your income tax, don't agree or sign a refund anticipation loan. Some preparers call them "rapid refunds." Sounds great, but you are losing money by paying a very high interest rate plus fees. The firms granting the loans make millions. Many taxpayers are unaware their rapid refund is a loan. You do financially better to wait the 3-4 weeks for the IRS to mail your refund.

"I THINK YOU'LL FIND SIR, OUR BROCHURE SAYS SAFE BEACH...YOU MUST HAVE GONE INTO THE WATER!"

Caution in the Car Lot

For the Federal Trade Commission online guide *Financing or Leasing a Car,* visit www.consumer .ftc.gov/articles/0056-financing-or-leasing-car or call 202-452-3245. Although the rules are helpful, you should understand the basic facts of auto leasing. It is rarely a sound financial move.

When you lease a car, you spend less on a monthly basis than you would buying a car. But at the end of the lease, you don't own a car. Businesses use this arrangement for income tax deductions, but the rest of us cannot.

There are two cheaper ways to buy a car. Buy an affordable car and keep it for at least one year after it's paid off, or look for a good used car.

Financing: Be Careful

Be aware that a car dealer may charge a markup for arranging your financing. You'll be repaying this through your monthly payments. Before buying:

- Check the current rates offered at a bank, a credit union or on the Internet.

- Ask credit agencies for a consumer credit history.

- Note the annual percentage rate the dealer offers, not just the monthly payments.

- Bargain for a lower rate; the dealer sets it, and it can be changed.

- Never sign a blank loan document or a blank check.

Used Car Purchases

A car has depreciated to half of its original value after two years but may still have three-quarters of its life left. The perils that confront the buyer in this field are so numerous that we hesitate to make recommendations. When buying a used car, be wary.

Check your Blue Book. Determine the kind of car you want to buy. Find the car you want, and have it checked by an independent mechanic. Check the car's maintenance record. Check www.carfax.com for a detailed vehicle history.

Shop for competitive deals, then get the car for the best price you can obtain from the dealer. Doing business with a reputable used car dealer that has been in business for a long time and has established a record for honesty and service may be the **best** advice.

Health Care Hazards

Americans spend $500 million yearly on vitamins, minerals, and health remedies *they don't need*. The Food and Drug Administration emphasizes that sensible eating can provide most of the nutrients the body needs, and everyday, cheaper foods may be as healthy as so-called health foods.

Americans are vulnerable to health swindles because we are health-conscious. We have come to think of science as achieving all of its goals. It must have found a remedy for our ailment.

The American Medical Association suggests that you can recognize a quack by any of the following:

■ Relies on a "special" formula or "secret" device to effect a cure.

■ Implies a quick or easy cure.

■ Relies heavily on testimonials from patients.

■ Will not allow methods to be examined by competent medical authorities.

■ Scoffs at the practice of medicine and claims of being persecuted by medical authorities.

■ Claims that methods are superior to those used by medical doctors.

The American Medical Association recommends the following to protect you from fraud:

■ Leave your diagnosis to your physician.

■ Take medications only under the prescription of your physician.

■ Be wary about testimonials. Even genuine cures may not be due to the causes held responsible for them. Spontaneous remission may account for relief that is supposed to have come from another source.

HIRING A CONTRACTOR

Get recommendations. Get at least 3 written estimates. Check contractor complaint records. Make sure the contractor meets insurance, licensing and registration requirements. Understand your payment options. Do not make a final payment or sign a final release until you are satisfied with the work and that the subcontractors and suppliers have been paid.

■ Beware of "sure cures" for ailments such as arthritis, for which no known cure has been found.

■ Avoid products that promise more than temporary relief for minor arthritis pains.

■ Check all medications with your physician before taking them.

■ Consult your pharmacist about how to take your medication and other drug information.

Stretching Health Care $$$

You should not skimp on your health care, but there are steps you can take to reduce health care costs. Consider the following:

■ Ask your doctor to write your prescription in generic terms. This can be much cheaper than buying brand names of the same medicine.

■ Call to consult about minor health problems.

■ Know which public health services are available for screening and detection of diseases.

■ Find out about free clinics operated by service-oriented agencies.

■ Avoid confinement in the hospital for diagnostic tests and treatment that could be given as an outpatient.

■ Do not insist on a private room.

■ Investigate the possibility of having the services of a visiting nurse before going to the hospital.

Room and board are cheaper at home than at the hospital if all you need is medical attention.

- Research group purchasing plans available to unions, consumer cooperatives and senior citizens.

Save on Vitamins and Medicines

Many of us need medicines and vitamins. They can be expensive. Some suggestions:

- Review medication with your doctor, if you are not getting results, to evaluate whether it is still needed or if there are any drug interactions.
- Shop around. Prices vary from pharmacy to pharmacy for the same medicines.
- Ask for a senior discount.
- Check Internet and mail-order pharmacies.
- If you take a drug regularly, check with your insurance plan to see if you get a 90-day supply of your medication or if they offer a mail-order discount option.
- Check the pharmacy industry's site at www.pparx.org for eligible programs.

Success: Without Really Trying

Your income in retirement is less than it was before retirement. You would welcome the additional security that the provision of more income, or the protection against greater expense, would afford. Many unscrupulous operators are ready to take advantage of the vulnerable position of the aged by offering a lot for a little.

The following have frequently been traps into which many individuals have fallen:

- **Work-at-home:** These opportunities appear in the newspaper and usually are designed to sell the products that are to be the basis of the lucrative home industry. Sometimes a registration fee is required, after which the applicant is advised that his products do not measure up to the high standards of the promoter.

  The Better Business Bureau warns against the following tactics:

  (a) Help-wanted ads with no offer of employment.

  (b) Offer of huge profits.

  (c) Emphasis on large, part-time earnings.

  (d) Use of testimonials with no way to check with the individuals.

  (e) Sell materials, kits, instructions, and equipment at high prices.

  (f) Guaranteed market.

  (g) Exaggerated demand for product.

  (h) Claim that no experience is necessary.

- **Purchase of franchise:** Ads used to offer great profits for little work. Exclusive territories, trained personnel to assist, and financial help is promised. Check with a bank, lawyer, and Better Business Bureau before investing money.

- **Chain-referral schemes:** This fraud consists of buying an expensive article with the hope that the purchase of similar articles by friends will result in commissions to reduce the original price.

- **Vanity publishers:** This fraud involves the publication of a book or recording music that you have written. Victims are led to believe that their works have merit and are encouraged to invest money in the publication or recording.

- **Land fraud:** The low price of a retirement home site should not make you less cautious about the purchase. Ask yourself these questions:

  (a) What taxes will have to be paid?

  (b) What about the title to the land? Is it clear?

  (c) Have I been pressured into making a quick decision?

  (d) Have I seen the land I want to buy?

  (e) Am I prepared to live in an isolated site, far from the city?

  (f) Is medical care available near the site?

  (g) Are utilities and facilities available?

  (h) How close will shopping facilities be?

  (i) *Before you buy or move, read Chapter 8.*

- **Debt consolidation:** where the consolidation fee is paid before money is applied to debts.

- **Charity rackets:**

  (a) Donate only to known causes and organizations.

  (b) Ask for a financial statement from unfamiliar organizations.

  (c) Check with the Better Business Bureau or Chamber of Commerce.

- **Fraudulent correspondence schools:** Watch the contract that must be signed, regardless of whether or not the individual wishes to continue with the course.

- **Memberships** in buyers, discount, recreational, or food distributors clubs, with representations that membership will result in savings.

The only protection you need is to be a little bit tougher. **Be hard to please. Insist on quality and service.** Don't believe everything you hear or read. Complain.

CONSUMER RESOURCES

USAGov Office of Products and Programs, 1800 F St., NW, Washington DC 20405, 844-872-4681 offers a *Consumer Information Catalog* that provides a directory of federal, state and local consumer offices, corporations' consumer offices, trade associations and dispute resolution programs. It highlights tips on how to use a credit card, complain about a defective product, select a financial institution and choose a school.

The Federal Trade Commission, www.ftc.gov, offers free resources with a broad range of federal information, resources and tips on consumer issues.

Know how and where to file a complaint when your rights as a consumer have been violated. **It is worth the bother.**

Many times you can go back to the person who is responsible for the unsatisfactory service or the sale of a faulty product, and a courteous request on your part is all that is necessary.

How to File a Complaint

When you report unsatisfactory goods or services, assemble all the information about dates, payments, contracts, receipts, etc., so that there is little room for confusion. You will also impress the individual that you are serious about carrying through with your complaint by going to all that trouble!

If you cannot get satisfaction from the salesperson, find the highest authority to which you can appeal in the store. Keep calm. Maintaining your composure will show that you are confident.

Letters should be written to the president of the company. State the facts clearly. Keep a copy of everything for your records.

For complaints that cannot be settled using these measures, contact your state attorney general's office. To file a complaint on financial matters with the Consumer Financial Protection Bureau, go to www.consumerfinance.gov/complaint or 855-411-2372.

> "The chief ingredient of fad diets is baloney."
>
> — *Neil Stone, MD*
>
> "Age is a question of mind over matter. If you don't mind, it doesn't matter."
>
> — *Satchel Paige*

You've Got Your Health

Much of life is improved by having good health. You may think that money is the most important part of retirement, but it is not. Your health is. If you are not healthy or able to enjoy activities, how much money you have becomes less important. An added benefit of good health is that your health costs are reduced, you are more productive at work and you can choose to work longer or have an active retirement. What are your chances of enjoying relatively good health during retirement?

George Gallup reported that 60% of those over 60 were able to physically do almost anything they wanted to do. There is good indication that many people are enjoying full and satisfying lives, usually with some reminder from their body that they are driving a model whose parts don't function as they did when they were brand new.

By age 45, most people have one or more chronic conditions. This number grows to 81%

by age 65. 49% reported some limitation of their activities due to these conditions, while only 16% reported major limitations.

You Are What You Eat

Proper diet will have some effect on your body and your frame of mind. A proper diet is one of the principal contributors to good health. Unfortunately, it is more difficult to maintain during the years when your body needs all the help it can get…during retirement.

Food is expensive, and the reduced budget on which you live may tempt you to cut corners at mealtime. Besides, your appetite is not what it once was, and you may have developed a dislike for certain foods. It's just too much bother to prepare food for just the two of you or just yourself.

PROFILE OF LONGEVITY

Individuals most likely to succeed at living a long time have:

- An understanding of themselves physically, mentally and socially
- Healthy eating habits
- Family meals
- Good medical care and regular medical, dental, and eye checkups—early and later in life
- Healthy attitudes—a sense of humor
- The ability to cope well with stress
- A habit of daily exercise
- Rewarding personal relationships
- A good environment—physically and mentally
- Good health habits and personal care
- A commitment to something other than themselves
- A willingness to try new things—a class, a musical instrument or a language
- Participation in religious activities or clubs
- Good genes

Examine your diet to see that it provides both the energy and the nutrients you need. Check our suggestions in Chapter Five for ways of doing this without spending more for food.

Take It Off

If a major problem is eating too much, it can be corrected by *eating less*. Not necessarily! A diet is a prescription for a particular physical condition. It should be given the same respect as any other medical recommendation. "One man's meat is another man's poison" is a way of reminding us that we each require *individual* diagnosis and prescription. Try to eat a balanced diet including foods low in saturated fats and cholesterol, lean meats, fruits, vegetables and foods with fiber such as grains and legumes.

About one older adult in three has a chronic health condition that requires a special diet. The most common diets limit the intake of salt, saturated fat and cholesterol. There is a relationship between weight and the number of diseases that are complicated by excess fat: the tendency toward heart attacks, cerebral hemorrhage, nephritis, and diabetes.

Diet counseling by a dietitian or nutritionist may be helpful in changing poor nutritional habits and adopting diets necessitated by disease. Insufficient exercise, diminished appetite, dental problems, gastrointestinal problems, being overweight or having heart disease and diabetes—Each makes specific diet changes necessary. About 50% of Americans have lost all their teeth by age 85.

Good eating habits, including proper diet, could cut heart and vascular diseases by 25%. A decrease in respiratory diseases by 20% and in arthritis and diabetes by 50% could be achieved by proper nutrition.

Don't Just Sit There!

Your health can determine both your quality of life and finances in retirement. You can improve your health with a fitness routine. Exercise is a vital necessity *every day*. You may be able to store the benefits of eating, but the benefits of exercise cannot be stored for long periods.

A physical fitness program has two goals: *organic fitness*, which includes the condition of the vital organs and limbs, and *dynamic fitness*, the efficiency of your heart and lungs.

You will be able to tell when your physical fitness program is having its desired effect. People around you will also be able to tell! Your attitude will be more positive and optimistic; you will accomplish more with less strain and tension.

When your body is functioning properly, you will have greater stamina, strength, endurance and coordination. And your joints! How stiff they are after extended periods of inactivity: long

trips, watching TV, etc. Regular exercise can bring back increased flexibility to most joints. For women, exercise decreases calcium loss from bones, thereby helping to prevent osteoporosis. An improved and more efficient circulatory system is another product of a good exercise program.

Chronic fatigue may be due to other causes, but much tiredness can be eliminated by greater activity.

The latest guidelines from federal health authorities and fitness experts stress that although strenuous exercise (such as jogging or cycling) provides the most benefits, more moderate exercise and even everyday physical activities (gardening, house cleaning, walking to work, or climbing a flight or two of stairs) can also help keep you healthy.

Exercise reduces the number of calories stored in your body as fat, keeping weight down and fitness up.

At Ease!

Don't overdo exercise, particularly at the beginning. It took more than a day to get in your present condition, and it may take a while before you begin to look and feel better. Make your routine reasonable and fun. Join a group. Your local Y, high school or college may have an adult program. Persuade a friend to walk with you, or get out and exercise with your dog. Find an exercise show on TV, or do exercises while watching the news. Things may sound better with your circulation tuned up! Exercise is the conditioner for the healthy and therapy for the ill.

Turn Back the Years...

So you don't enjoy jogging miles every day—or you can't. You don't get a kick out of exhausting yourself on a tennis court. In fact, you don't do much of anything that involves physical exertion.

You have a problem, but fortunately it is one that can be solved easily and without cost, through regular exercise. As you grow older, exercise becomes more vital. "Exercise is the closest thing we have to a Fountain of Youth," says Marie Bernard of the National Institute of Aging. "Take advantage of exercise to improve the quality of a longer life." People who engage in moderate exercise at least 3 to 5 times a week can reduce their blood pressure by an average of 10 points and dramatically lower their risk of diabetes.

A study of 300,000 men over 45 years old found that the death rate among those leading completely sedentary lives was four to five times that of men who exercise regularly. The study confirmed that bodies deteriorate—both men's and women's—without proper exercise. This is so whether you are in your 20s or up in your 70s or 80s. Bodies must be used. If they aren't, they lose efficiency and tone.

You can delay or reverse many of the deteriorating effects of age by exercising—alone,

or with your spouse or a buddy. All it takes is determination. It can be as easy and enjoyable as a half-hour walk four times a week.

As You Grow Older

Dr. Herbert A. de Vries, director of the exercise laboratory of the Andrus Gerontology Center of the University of Southern California, outlined what happens to your body as you age and how regular exercise can help in coping with changes:

- The heart's ability to pump blood declines by about 8% each decade in adulthood, and blood pressure increases as fatty deposits clog arteries. By middle age, the openings of the coronary arteries are likely to be about 29% smaller than when you were in your mid-20s.

- Lung capacity decreases and the chest wall stiffens as you grow older; this cuts the amount of oxygen available to body tissues for work and other physical activities. The amount of oxygen you must use at age 75 is ordinarily less than half what it was at 20.

- Skeletal muscles, such as those in arms and legs, gradually lose strength. Tests show that 3% to 5% of muscle tissue is lost every decade. Loss of muscular strength and tissue means ebbing endurance.

- The proportion of your body that is fat increases. To keep the same proportion of fat to lean body mass (not the way you look outside, but internally) you have to weigh less and less as you grow older.

Don't let these facts about aging worry you too much! Using your body can mitigate and delay the aging processes. Keeping active will help you stay young in spite of your calendar years and will help you feel better also.

Enhance Your Vigor

Exercise can enhance the body's vigor and increase its work capacity. It can help the heart deliver more blood and oxygen for body tissues, slow the conversion of lean body mass to fat, and strengthen bones. It tends to stave off the aging of nerve cells, and, according to some medical opinion, it can slow down or avert arthritic changes in hips, knees and other joints. Exercise can improve movement and balance and reduce the risk of falling.

Don't forget an exercise you do—or should do—every day: *walking*. Walking provides excellent exercise for the heart, muscles and lungs and can have added benefits as well. Walking can give you a chance to relax, enjoy your surroundings and give you a much-needed "breath of fresh air." Build up your walking distance slowly, keeping your pace fast without becoming winded. Increase the distance you walk until you think you have exercised enough—45 minutes is a good limit for many people. Be sure to wear a good pair of sneakers that fit well.

Get Moving...But Wisely

We would all like to feel better and have our bodies be their best. What comes easiest for most of us is a regimen of regular exercise in the home to tone muscles, prevent sagging posture, and keep the heart strong and the joints flexible. Such a routine can be highly effective and, once you get into the swing of it, enjoyable and relaxing.

A word of caution: Whatever you do, especially if you are over 40, should be undertaken with medical advice. This is critical if an exercise program or involvement in a sport is strenuous, and it is important even for an exercise program in the home. Your doctor may want to suggest special exercises for you or caution you against undertaking too much.

Your Home Routine

Exercise or physical fitness programs can be worked out for anyone—the middle-aged, the healthy aging and those with special health needs. Sit-down exercises for those in wheelchairs or who are otherwise sedentary are particularly important, as are exercises for the bedridden.

The Maryland Commission on Physical Fitness, with the National Association for Human Development and the Maryland Office on Aging, has developed a fitness program called "The Basic Ten."

The Basic Ten...

1 **Arm Swings**—Swing right arm, rotating forward 5 times; reverse motion, rotating backward 5 times. Repeat with left arm. With both arms together in a windmill fashion, swing forward 5 times.

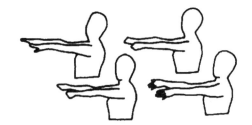

2 **Finger Squeeze**—Extend arms shoulder height in front, palms down; squeeze the fingers slowly, then release. Repeat 5 times. Then turn palms up; squeeze fingers 5 times. Extend arms again in front, and shake fingers 5 times.

3 **Arm Turns**—Extend arms to the side, palms up, cup hands, turn arms down in a circular movement and return to starting position. Repeat 5 times. Extend arms, cup hands, facing down, turn arms in the opposite direction 5 times.

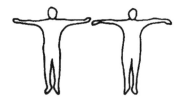

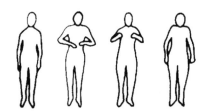

4 **Shoulder Rolls**—Beginning with arms at side, roll shoulders forward in full circle, slowly, 5 times; reverse by rolling shoulders backward in a circle, slowly, 5 times. Then shrug shoulders up and down 5 times.

5 **Body Stretch**—Extend right foot forward as far as it will go, leaving the left foot firmly planted; bend body forward with arms extended, stretch forward 5 counts, stretching further forward on each count. Reverse procedure. Lift up on your toes, stretch overhead to a count of 5.

...for Physical Fitness

Head and Neck Exercise—Place hands on hips. Bend forward so that chin touches the chest. Then bend head to starting position, and slowly turn the head to the left; return head to starting position, and then slowly turn head to the right. Repeat 5 times.

6

7 **Easy Back Stretch**—Sit partway off the seat of a straight chair. Relax your body, and let your head drop between your knees. Your shoulders should rest on your knees; your hands will hang alongside your legs. *Breathe naturally* while you relax in this position for two or three minutes. Then bring your hands up to your knees again and, *using your arms for support,* begin to curl yourself up to a sitting position, with your head straightening last.

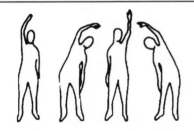

Body Side Stretch—Place left hand on left hip, extend right arm over head, and bend to left side toward the ground, to the count of two. Return to starting position and place right hand on right hip, with left arm extended upward over head, and bend to the right, to the count of two.

8

9 **Posture Exercise**—Stand erect with feet about six inches apart. Tighten leg muscles, tighten stomach by drawing it in, extend chest, bring arms up with clenched fists chest high, take deep breath, let it out slowly (keeping the muscles taut and rigid) and vibrate arms back for a count of three.

Arm Stretch—With feet six inches apart, make fists, bend elbows, then thrust arms forward and bring them back; thrust sideways, bring back, then thrust arms upward and down. Repeat 3 times.

10

The Basic Ten

Before beginning the Basic Ten:

- **See your doctor first.**

- Warm up before exercising. Breathe deeply, rising up on your toes slowly, with arms extended over your head, then exhale slowly. Three times should do it. Also walk in place, lifting knees high ten times.

- Do your exercises slowly, and do not do too much for too long at first. *Stop* if you begin hurting anywhere or get tired. Increase your regimen gradually.

- Take deep breaths between exercises.

- If you feel some dizziness, you can avoid it by resting before alternating sides in an exercise.

- **15 to 20 minutes a day** will give you a good workout. Lie flat after each workout, and take 15 minutes of yoga-like exercises: stretching leg muscles by bending legs from the hip and knee, tensing them as much as you can and holding them down with your arms.

Now, take a look at the Basic Ten. Good luck, and happy exercising!

An Apple a Day, Plus...

Good nutrition is the cornerstone of a happy, healthy life and is instrumental in disease prevention and control. Preventative health measures include more than the regular consumption of apples. There are precautions we can take to reduce the probability that we will lose our health through sickness or accidents. We can increase our resistance to illness and make early detection and treatment work against many disabilities.

For a Good Night's Sleep

What time you get there isn't as important as how long you stay there. Individual requirements differ, but 7-8 hours during a 24-hour period is about average. Scientists have observed that cumulative sleep loss can lead to nervousness and psychosomatic illness. Chronic inability to sleep suggests the need for a doctor's attention. *Too much sleep* can be a problem, indicating boredom or illness.

If you are more than occasionally experiencing trouble falling asleep and sleeping well, if it is a frequently recurring, long-lasting chronic problem that you can't shake, see your doctor. It is better to be assured that you haven't anything to worry about than to find out later that you have a problem that requires professional treatment.

Hazards to Good Sleep

Drs. Joyce and Anthony Kales, who conducted sleep research at the Hershey Medical Center of Pennsylvania State University, have found that many chronic insomniacs keep their problems bottled up inside, without venting anger, frustrations and disappointments.

According to the Kales, tension, stress and anxiety build-up are carried into the night. They are likely to cause racing thoughts, activate the physical arousal system and make it difficult to get to sleep.

Chronic insomnia often can be traced to illnesses such as angina, asthma or other respiratory disorders or to back problems or arthritis. If you suffer persistent sleeplessness, see your doctor. Prescribed medication often helps.

Here are some suggestions outlined by Dr. Donald Douglas of the Lenox Hill Hospital in New York, Drs. Joyce and Anthony Kales of the Pennsylvania Hershey Medical Center, Wallace Mendelson of the National Institute of Mental Health and others in the field:

- Recognize that sleep needs differ; you may be among those who need less than a seven-and-one-half-hour norm.

- Go to bed and get up about the same time every day, weekends included.

- If you go to bed and don't feel sleepy, try to lull yourself to sleep with a book that isn't so absorbing that it keeps you awake. Or turn on quiet, soothing music.

- Avoid or limit coffee, tea or other caffeine products and nicotine in the afternoon or evening. Alcohol may help you go to sleep, but it can cause recurring awakenings.

- Do not exercise rigorously within 5 to 6 hours of bedtime.

- Do not eat heavy meals in the evening, and drink fewer liquids.

- Do not watch TV in bed.

- Drink warm milk. It has an essential amino acid that has been used medically to treat depression and as a sedative. Although milk has only a small amount of amino acid (medically referred to as L-tryptophan), it often helps assure restful sleep. Some drinks, like a "hot toddy," may help you fall asleep, but the sleep you get will be less restful. It is best to avoid alcohol before heading to bed.

- Relax in bed and try to be absolutely still. Because the body naturally resists non-movement, each time one moves, in trying to find a sleep-inducing position, one must start over again to relax the body and the mind.

- Concentrate on breathing, inhaling and exhaling deeper and at regular intervals; think of your breathing, trying to keep your mind clear of disturbing thoughts; your grandmother probably called this "counting sheep."

- Don't try to force sleep. The more you struggle to sleep, or worry about wakefulness, the harder it will be to get to sleep. It can be better to relax and stay awake a while longer.

- Don't resort to pills *unless* they've been prescribed by your doctor. Though over-the-counter remedies to promote quick sleep and restful nights can be useful for occasional sleeplessness, the National Institutes of Health has warned that sleeping pills, or even mild remedies, can be harmful if overused. If you can tolerate aspirin, you might try it as a relaxant at bedtime, when you need one.

For more information and brochures on sleep difficulties, write to: The National Sleep Foundation, 1010 N Glebe Road, Suite 420, Arlington, VA 22201, 703 243-1697, or on the internet: www.sleepfoundation.org.

Stop Smoking

Smokers are becoming a minority—Only one-third of adults are now cigarette smokers. If you still smoke, now's the time to join the more than 30 million ex-smokers. Smoking is an expensive habit, both in terms of your health and your wealth. It's responsible for more cancer-related deaths than any other single agent, and it's a contributing factor in emphysema, bronchitis and heart attack.

You know you should quit. Let's accentuate the positive. Think of the benefits of quitting now.

When you quit smoking, your body starts to repair itself almost immediately. You enter lower risk groups. You lose your smoker's hacking cough and related head and stomach aches. You recover your sense of taste and smell. Smoking is one habit you can afford to lose.

The American Cancer Society has information to help you. Contact your local chapter.

ZZZZZZZZZZZZZ • DO'S AND DONT'S ABOUT SLEEP!

Warning of a Stroke

Knowing the warning signs and getting quick treatment is critical to treating a stroke. Stroke is the third leading cause of death and the number one cause of adult disability.

- Unexplained weakness, tingling or numbness in the face, arm or leg, usually on one side of the body.
- Difficulty speaking or understanding words.
- Changes in vision such as blurred or decreased vision.
- Severe headache, sometimes with nausea or vomiting.
- Dizziness or difficulty with walking or coordination.

If you or anyone has any of these symptoms call 911 immediately.

Mental and Physical Health

Mental and physical conditions are too complicated to discuss at length in this chapter. Most of us have sensed the effect that illness in one area has upon well-being in the other. The person with a healthy self-concept and social adjustment will not be completely protected from poor health. But those who cope successfully with life's problems, not only during aging but throughout all of life, usually are more positive about themselves. Just as you have probably faced crises or problematic situations during your life, you will face them in retirement and cope with them as effectively as you did earlier.

Profile of a Healthy Life

People with the following traits tend to adjust and cope better than those who lack them. Check those that describe you:

- ❏ Enduring and honest affection for others
- ❏ Independent
- ❏ Has satisfying outlets for time and energy
- ❏ Enjoys life
- ❏ Has a sense of usefulness

- ❏ Avoids self-pity

Individuals who have good social relationships tend to live longer than those who don't.

Additional Supports

People who add additional meaning to their lives can draw from these resources during tough times. Some individuals develop meaning through their life experiences and communities, which can include church communities, social clubs, volunteer organizations, places of higher learning, senior centers and more.

Many adults choose to perform volunteer work each year, and studies suggest such activities are good for the individual as well as for the community. Research has indicated that volunteering can improve a person's quality of life and create meaningful relationships. For a further discussion of volunteer options such as helping in after-school programs, participating in religious organizations, donating time in nursing homes or hospitals, repairing community playgrounds or sponsoring youth activities, see Chapter 11.

Living With Stress

Stress is the body's physical and chemical reaction to anything that frightens, excites, confuses or endangers a person.

No matter what you do on the job or away from it, you may come under mental or physical stress. Although stress is not necessarily a medical problem, it can be. It must be watched.

Tolerable stress promotes physical and mental development and growth. The adrenaline pumped into the bloodstream at such times can give the extra strength needed to achieve more—to endure more, work harder and work more creatively.

Studies conducted by the Harvard University Medical School, Boston University and Northwestern University found strong evidence that prolonged and excessive stress can be a serious health concern—even a killer. It can make men and women more susceptible to a wide variety of diseases, including cancer.

To reduce stress in your life, maintain a healthy weight, get rest, cut down on caffeine, drink water, eat right, and get 30 minutes of exercise a day. The mood-boosting effects of moderate to brisk aerobic activity may last up to 12 hours, say researchers at the University of Vermont. "Even a few minutes a day can pay off," says Dr. Jeremy Sibold. Pick any activity you enjoy, and do it as often as possible.

The Blahs...or Worse

In its milder forms, stress usually leads to nothing worse than a persistent case of the "blahs," or general unhappiness, depression and nagging anxieties. The serious problems come when *stress* is allowed to become *distress*—when the body and mind no longer can handle it. When this happens, it becomes a potential medical problem.

Stress can cause changes in the body's immune system and reduce the body's ability to fight virus-infected cells. According to Harvard's Dr. Steve Locke, this can "predispose a person to illness."

Stress affects the old and the young, but because the young usually have more physical resilience, they are better able to cope with it. Those approaching retirement and retirees are the most vulnerable.

As we grow older, says Dr. Ruth B. Weg of the University of Southern California's Andrus Gerontology Center, we have "a diminishing ability to respond to stress." It hits harder, and recovery takes longer.

We must watch ourselves more closely as we grow older and learn to recognize the symptoms of stress. Learn to cope with stress before it builds up dangerously.

Recognizing the Symptoms

Unfortunately, too many of us do not recognize the signs of stress or pay too little attention to them. For far too many, it's a natural part of the wear and tear of life—something that must be endured.

Recognizing the signs of stress is the first step toward coping with it effectively.

What are the symptoms? "Butterflies" in the stomach. Tension and nervousness over prolonged

A GOOD LAUGH

Laugh more; at least once a day, get a good laugh. According to Michael Miller, director of Preventive Cardiology at the University of Maryland Medical Center, it helps keep the blood vessels dilated and protects against heart attacks.

periods. Light perspiration when things don't seem to be going right. Headaches. A feeling of pressure on the back of the neck. Heavy breathing. Or an "internal racing" and pounding heart.

We may be alerted to stress by insomnia, ulcers and other stomach troubles. We may find it's the cause of hypertension and heart strain or a change to an unhealthy pattern of behavior, such as excessive smoking, drinking or eating in search of relief. A sudden urge for snacking could signal stress! Recognize that stress is a problem that must be dealt with, to minimize the way it affects you.

How to Ease Stress

Start by seeking the cause of stress. Often it's obvious. Sometimes it isn't.

The death or serious illness of a spouse is considered by psychologists to be the most serious cause of stress. On a scale of 100, other causes are rated substantially lower.

The loss of a spouse, or the death of a close relative or friend, is the hardest to handle. Help should be sought.

Other major causes of stress include retirement (rated high on the stress scale because of the upheaval it causes in personal lives), illness and accidents, marital troubles and divorce, sexual difficulties, financial problems, job worries, work-related problems and changes in living conditions.

Unlike the death of a spouse, these are seldom serious enough, alone, to cause major problems. When one stressful situation comes, others often follow. The loss of a job, 47 on the stress scale, can cause financial problems, disrupt living patterns and lead to all sorts of satellite problems, sending the stress count above 200—a critical level.

Studies that have concentrated on the causes of serious stress have found that 27% of a group interviewed intensively had experienced "high levels of psychic distress" over a year's time as a result of a steady buildup of stress.

Stress takes two basic forms: Mental stress and physical stress.

- Mental stress is a "bad" stress, caused primarily by emotional disturbances, frustrations or anxieties—things over which we have little or no control. These feelings of stress can be serious and need prompt attention.

- Physical stress is a "good" stress, as long as you don't overexert yourself. While it can be serious in later years, it can also be relaxing and an antidote for mental stress.

Rest is good in cases of physical stress—but physical activity, even to a point of careful stress, is helpful when mental stress is a problem. Don't sit and worry; do something involving physical activity.

Stress: Work It Off

In retirement, recognize that boredom from inactivity is stressful; work it off. Everyday activities such as gardening, chores around the home, walking or a physical hobby will suffice. Exertion is not always necessary. The concentration needed for chess or some other game, a crossword puzzle or reading can help.

Often, simply blowing off steam can help relieve stress. Repressed anger, frustration and anxiety make it build up in daily life. Some therapists advocate going into a room, closing doors and windows, and letting off a "primal scream" to ease pressures. That sounds extreme. Find your own way, but get rid of stress—and develop ways to avoid its return.

Stress that leads to muscular contractions and aches and tension headaches can be eased by medication, usually aspirin if you can take it, but don't be a pill-popper. Medication may ease stress symptoms, but it does not attack the cause of the stress, and it can be habit-forming and lead to a different form of personal stress.

Consider aspirin or anti-depressant or anti-anxiety drugs (they should be prescribed by a doctor) as only temporary relief for stress. Seek real relief, not from pills, but from the causes of the stress you feel.

Rest is important to relieve physical stress. It can also be important in situations involving mental and emotional stress: Lack of sleep or rest aggravates tensions and the body's ability to throw them off. However, sleep does not necessarily attack the causes of stress; the tension headaches or tight muscles you have at bedtime often return after you awaken.

WHAT YOU CAN DO WHEN YOU FEEL STRESS COMING ON!

TEST YOUR STRESS LEVEL

Score Yourself: Never = 0; Seldom = 1; Frequently = 2

How often do you feel:

Strong anxiety . . . . ( )
Irritable over little things . . . . ( )
Frustrated . . . . ( )
Quick anger . . . . ( )
A desire to avoid people. . . . . ( )
A difficulty in concentrating . . . . ( )
Easily disturbed or startled. . . . . ( )
Jittery, unable to sit still . . . . ( )
Unusually emotional . . . . ( )
Depressed. . . . . ( )
A loss of interest in everything . . . . ( )
Persistently keyed up . . . . ( )

How often do you experience:

General fatigue. . . . . ( )
Sleeplessness at night. . . . . ( )
Heart pounding. . . . . ( )
Headaches . . . . ( )
Breathing difficulties . . . . ( )
Burping, gassiness, acid stomach. . . . . . . ( )
Frequent need to urinate. . . . . ( )
Tense head and neck muscles . . . . ( )
Grinding of teeth . . . . ( )
Dry mouth or throat . . . . ( )
Sudden perspiration . . . . ( )
Cold hands or feet if it's warm,
 sweaty hands or feet otherwise . . . . ( )

Add the point totals in the two columns: If together they are 10 or under, you are normal; if 10 to 20, take care; if higher, you could have a problem.

Stress also leads to night wakefulness. If you can't get the seven or eight hours of sleep you need, consult your doctor.

If you can isolate what is bothering you, the cause of your stress, try to work out a solution. If there are a number of causes, work on them one at a time, the most important first. Learn to accept what you cannot change, problems beyond your control, until you are better able to do something about them.

If you can't seem to work things out on your own, talk to a sympathetic listener, someone you respect and trust. It will help put things in better perspective. The listener can be a member of your family, a friend, a clergyman or teacher, someone in the personnel office, or your doctor.

Serious Stress: Talk It Out

If professional counseling seems wise, there are family service and other similar agencies available.

Don't feel ashamed, embarrassed or guilty about going to a professional for assistance; it's not an admission of personal inadequacy but a mark of intelligence to seek advice. Dr. Locke of Harvard says, "To the extent that an individual has effective coping strategies and social psychological resources to rely on, stress should cause less deterioration of health and well-being."

When Stress Builds Up

Try to relax. Slow down: Don't rush your life away. As a cardiologist put it, don't let yourself become a heart-attack-prone person—one who is hurried, aggressive, impatient and easily angered. A more relaxed person lives a far more pleasant and healthier life.

Rid yourself of trivial obligations. Concentrate on what is most important to you. Cultivate diversions, such as: exercise, concerts, museums and visits with friends. Learn to enjoy your own company. Do nothing rather than rush to keep up with a full calendar.

Learn a few secrets that can help fight stress. One is a simple breathing exercise. When you feel stress coming on, take a slow breath and exhale slowly, a count of four in, four out, and repeat. As you exhale, let your body go limp. Let your mind relax.

Another technique is the rag doll exercise. Sit on the edge of a straight chair, knees about 12 inches apart, legs in front of the chair. Sit straight and then collapse forward, back rounded, hands resting on your knees. Let your mind concentrate on parts of your body, relaxing each in turn, breathing deeply.

You should feel better once you learn to relax completely. Do these whenever you feel a need to ease body tensions.

Coping With Depression

You hear people say: "I've got a bad case of the blues" or "I'm down deep in the dumps." Chances are you've said it also. It happens to everyone.

If it is a mood that comes and goes, you can fight it off by thinking and acting positively. If it doesn't go away, you should be aware that depression can be a major mental health problem.

It affects more than your mood. It can manifest itself in symptoms as diverse as sleeplessness (you lie awake worrying about real or fancied problems), boredom, inertia, an inability to concentrate, impatience, irritability and, not uncommonly, stress. It can affect your appetite; you might lose interest in food.

It can lead to more smoking or drinking. It can be a factor in driving. Accident records indicate that drivers suffering from depression are more likely to be reckless and to lack the concentration vital for safety. It can affect performance on the job.

The Blues or Depression

New York University's Medical Center has conducted intensive research into depression, resulting in more accurate diagnoses and more effective treatments.

Irene Chang, coordinator of the depression studies program, has circulated a checklist of possible symptoms for the early recognition of depression problems.

Symptoms of depression include:

- ❏ A low mood: feeling sad, blue and/or hopeless much of the time.
- ❏ Appetite disturbance: a poor appetite or an increased appetite.
- ❏ Sleep problems: difficulty falling asleep, waking up during the night or waking early.
- ❏ Lack of energy: quickly fatigued, tired for no reason, tense, with difficulty relaxing.
- ❏ Loss of interest in usual activities.
- ❏ Feelings of self-reproach or inappropriate guilt.
- ❏ Trouble concentrating and possible difficulties making decisions.
- ❏ Excessive thoughts of death or that life is not worth living.

If you checked off four or more, see a physician. Approximately 19 million Americans are afflicted with depression every year.

Exercise is also helpful in fighting depression. Try to engage in an exercise that you enjoy for at least 20 minutes a day. Be sure to check with your doctor before starting any exercise program.

The Blues...Get Rid of Them

The symptoms for the plain old blues or blahs are much the same as those for more serious forms of depression. The big difference is how frequently they recur and in how many ways.

Millions of Americans suffer now and then from the blues. However, in most instances you can fight off the blues. It's not always easy. You have to concentrate on positive thinking instead of worrying about troubles you can do nothing about.

NYU's Depression Studies Program suggests:

- Don't knock yourself.
- Don't build up a problem by going over it time and again; you'll make it worse, not better.
- Share your feelings with others; your spouse, a relative, a friend or a consultant is likely to have good advice.
- Don't use your age as an excuse for being down, mentally or physically.
- Give yourself credit for what you've accomplished through the years—and what you can continue to contribute.
- If your blues are about retiring, get rid of them; approach retirement positively as something you can make comfortable and happy.

COMMUNICATION

Good communication with your doctor improves health outcomes, satisfaction and a motivation to change unhealthy behaviors. Go to the appointment with questions. Tell your doctor the truth.

Doctor's Visit

According to the American Society of Internal Medicine, 70% of a correct diagnosis depends on what the patient tells the doctor. It is important to have clear communications.

To make the most of your doctor visits:

- Report health concerns.
- Freely exchange information, and ask questions.
- To prevent drug interaction: Tell your doctor and pharmacist all the medications (prescription and over the counter) and dietary supplements that you take.
- Prepare your questions before your visit.
- Have your files ready when seeing a new doctor.
- If possible, bring a spouse, family or friend with you to the visit; ask them to take notes while you listen to the doctor.
- Ask the doctor when you should take your medicine and about possible side effects.
- Participate in treatment choices.
- Ask the doctor to explain medical jargon.
- Have the doctor summarize the visit.

HEALTH & RETIREMENT

According to EBRI, more than half of the people who retired earlier than they planned did so because of health reasons. Now is the time to take steps to stay or to get healthy. The National Institutes of Health cites that losing weight can improve your blood pressure, cholesterol and blood sugar. Eat healthy meals, maintain a healthy weight, get moving, take your medications and find ways to relieve stress.

Checklist
for Health

Do you—

Yes	No	
❑	❑	Eat a balanced diet: milk, milk products, meat, poultry, fish, fruits, vegetables and grains?
❑	❑	Limit salt, sugar, fat and red meat?
❑	❑	Limit coffee and alcohol to two drinks per day?
❑	❑	Make mealtime a pleasure?
❑	❑	Control weight and exercise regularly?
❑	❑	Not smoke?
❑	❑	Sleep well?
❑	❑	Relax easily and laugh frequently?
❑	❑	Have stress under control?
❑	❑	Control medication?
❑	❑	Keep a list of your medications and bring it with you on your doctor visits?
❑	❑	Have your bone density screened?
❑	❑	Have a stable emotional life?
❑	❑	Have your vision checked every year?
❑	❑	Participate in community activities?
❑	❑	Have regular check-ups? Come prepared with written concerns and questions?
❑	❑	Know which hospital emergency room is best for your particular condition?
❑	❑	Keep mentally active: reading, studying, attending discussions and cultural events?
❑	❑	Wash your hands?
❑	❑	Tell your doctor your family health history?
❑	❑	Ask about possible side effects of proposed treatments or medications?
❑	❑	Know that exercise is the single best thing you can do for your brain in terms of mood, memory and learning?
❑	❑	Check the FTC's website to find information on health topics? Go to www.consumer.ftc.gov/health.
❑	❑	Review your medication's safety alerts, generic equivalents and information on prescription and over-the-counter drugs? Check www.fda.gov/drugs and click "Search Drugs@FDA" under "Spotlight."

"If I knew I was going to live this long, I'd have taken better care of myself."

— *Mickey Mantle*

"The first wealth is health."

— *Ralph Waldo Emerson*

Medicare

Medicare is a government-sponsored health insurance program available to Americans 65 and older, severely disabled persons under 65, those with end-stage renal disease, and those who become disabled due to ALS or asbestos-related lung disease from Libby, Montana. Medicare has two parts: hospital insurance (Medicare Part A) and medical insurance (Medicare Part B).

Medicare's hospital insurance component (Part A) covers a significant portion of hospitalization costs and also helps pay for certain follow-up care after you leave the hospital.

Note: Although full retirement age for Social Security benefits is increasing, Medicare is still available at age 65.

Medicare Part B Insurance

Traditional Medicare Part B medical insurance is a fee-for-service program. Medicare pays for 80% of the approved amount for the cost of the service;

you pay the remaining 20% (there is a $185 annual deductible). Under traditional Medicare, doctors are restricted in how much they can charge Medicare patients (but they are not required to see Medicare patients).

Medicare Part B helps pay for laboratory tests, x-rays and some medical equipment that is necessary. Prescription medications are not covered under Medicare Part B, and screening tests, such as cholesterol testing, are not automatically covered. If you request screening tests or your doctor recommends them, you may be responsible for payment. Reimbursement for some screening tests is now available.

Enrollment Information

Hospital insurance (Medicare Part A) is available to anyone who is eligible for Social Security benefits. You do not have to retire to get hospital insurance. It is available **free** at age 65, **but you must enroll**. Check with your Social Security office **three months before** you reach age 65. People who have not worked long enough to qualify for Social Security can buy Medicare Part A insurance by paying a monthly premium.

Medical insurance (Medicare Part B) is available to anyone who is 65 or older. You pay a monthly premium. If you were covered for medical insurance by your employer while working and will still be covered in retirement, signing up for Medicare Part B insurance may not be necessary. You'll save the monthly premium.

Medical insurance has a 7-month initial enrollment period. This period begins **three months before** you turn 65. For example, if you turn 65 on April 11, the enrollment period begins January 1 and lasts until July 31. If you turn down medical insurance and then decide you want it after your 7-month initial enrollment period ends, you can sign up during a general enrollment period—January 1 through March 31 of each year. However, if you enroll during a general enrollment period, your medical insurance protection **won't start until the following July, and your premium will be 10% higher** for each 12-month period you could have been enrolled but were not.

Medicare (Part A) Hospital Insurance: Covered Services per Benefit Period‡

Service	Benefits‡	You Pay†
Hospitalization Semi-private room and board, general nursing, and miscellaneous hospital services and supplies	First 60 days 61st day to 90th day Lifetime reserve day*	$1,364 deductible $341 per day $682 per day
Post Hospital Skilled Nursing Facility Care In a facility approved by Medicare. You must have been in a hospital for at least 3 days and enter the facility within 30 days after hospital discharge§ and with the same diagnosis as leaving the hospital	First 20 days	Nothing
	21st to 100th day	$170.50 per day
	Beyond 100 days	All costs
Home Health Care Medicare pays intermittent visits for skilled nursing care or physical therapy	Unlimited visits as medically necessary	Nothing 20% of Medicare-approved amount for durable medical equipment
Hospice Care	Two 90-day periods and an unlimited number of 60-day periods	Co-payment of up to $5 for outpatient prescription drugs and 5% of the Medicare-approved amount for inpatient respite care
Blood	Blood	For the first 3 pints, then 20% of the Medicare-approved amount**

People not eligible for Social Security benefits can purchase Medicare Part A Hospital Insurance for $437 per month.
* 60 reserve days may be used only once: days used are not renewable.
† These figures are subject to change each year.
‡ A Benefit Period begins on the first day you receive service as an inpatient in a hospital and ends after you have been out of the hospital or skilled nursing facility for 60 days in a row.
§ Medicare and private insurance will not pay for most nursing home care. You pay for custodial care and most care in a nursing home. There are now some policies on the market which will pay for all nursing home costs, but they are very expensive.
** Medicare pays processing costs; if you have donors to replace the blood, it would cost you nothing.

Medicare (Part B) Medical Insurance: Covered Services per Benefit Year

Service	Benefits	You Pay*
Medical Expense Physician's services, inpatient and outpatient medical services and supplies, physical and speech therapy, ambulance, chiropractic (limited), occupational therapy, durable medical equipment, prosthetic devices, second opinion before surgery, podiatrist's services, diagnostic laboratory tests, etc.	Medicare pays for medical services in or out of the hospital. Some insurance policies pay less (or nothing) for hospital outpatient medical services or services in a doctor's office.	$185 deductible* plus 20% of balance (Plus any charge above approved amount)†
Home Health Care Intermittent visits for skilled nursing care or physical therapy	Unlimited visits as medically necessary	Nothing. 20% of the Medicare approved amount for durable medical equipment. There may be limits on therapy.
Outpatient Hospital Treatment	Unlimited as medically necessary	A coinsurance or co-payment amount that varies by service
Blood	Blood	For first 3 pints,‡ plus 20% of balance of approved amount

Available at a monthly premium in 2019:	You Pay	If Your 2017 Yearly Income and Filing Status Is (subject to change)	
		Single	Married
	$135.50	$85,000 or less	$170,000 or less
	$189.60	$85,001-$107,000	$170,001-$214,000
	$270.90	$107,001-$133,500	$214,001-$267,000
	$352.20	$133,501-$160,000	$267,001-$320,000
	$433.40	$160,001-$500,000	$320,001-$750,000
	$460.50	Above $500,000	Above $750,000

* Once you have paid $185 for covered services, the Part B deductible does not apply to further covered services the rest of the year.
† You pay for charges greater than the amount approved by Medicare, unless the doctor or supplier agrees to accept Medicare's approved amount as the total charge for services rendered. Always ask your doctor or supplier to accept assignment. Assignment means the doctor or supplier accepts as full payment whatever the Medicare allowed charge is and can bill you only the $185 deductible, if not already paid, plus the 20% co-insurance.
‡ There is only one deductible for blood each year. If you meet the blood deductible under Part A, you do not have to meet it again under Part B.

If you are age 65 or older and you or your spouse are still working and are receiving coverage through an employer or union (contact the administrator of the benefits to find how your insurance works with Medicare), you will need to enroll within 8 months of leaving the job to avoid the penalty.

Those who have opted for early retirement benefits under Social Security or Railroad Retirement are automatically enrolled in Medicare Part B when they reach age 65. Monthly premiums are deducted from Social Security checks.

Medigap Insurance Policies

It is important to note that Medicare Part A and Medicare Part B benefits **do not cover all health care costs**. In many cases, these additional costs can be quite substantial, which is why many insurance companies now offer Medigap policies covering costs not covered by Medicare. Medigap policies can no longer provide prescription drug coverage; if you have it now with your current policy, you can keep it, but most coverage is not considered creditable.

Medigap policies range in cost. All policies cover a basic core of services not paid in full by Medicare. More expensive policies may pay for doctor's charges above Medicare's proscribed amounts and other benefits you may or may not require.

You should review your Medigap policy each year. Medigap policies are sold by private

MEDICARE BENEFITS

With Medicare, you are able to get a yearly wellness visit and many preventive services for no fee. For all Medicare benefits, go to: www.medicare.gov. Also see *Medicare & You* 2019 at www.medicare.gov/pubs/pdf/10050-Medicare-and-You.pdf.

insurance companies and offer standardized benefits that are identified by letters in most states. Medigap Plans E, H, I, and J are no longer offered. If you are in these plans, you may keep them, but premiums are expected to rise since no new people are coming into the plans. Plans C and F will no longer be available as of January 1, 2020. New plans M and N have been added. **Shop around** and buy a policy that offers only what you need.

Although benefits are identical for Medigap plans of the same type, premiums may vary greatly from one company or area to another. Insurance companies use three different methods to calculate premiums: issue age, attained age and no age rating.

If your company uses the issue age method and you were 65 when you bought the policy, you will always pay the same premium the company charges people who are 65, regardless of your age. If it uses the attained age method, the premium is based on your current age and will increase as you grow older. Under the no age rating, everyone pays the same premium regardless of age. The insurance company can raise your premiums only when it has approval to raise the premiums for everyone else with the same policy.

If you have Medicare Advantage, you do not need a Medigap policy.

Important: You cannot be turned down for Medigap insurance if you apply within six months after you reach age 65. After that, insurers, with certain important exceptions, may turn you down (see HMO Concerns pages 69–70).

Check with the Centers for Medicare and Medicaid Services at 877-910-7579 or www.medigap.com.

MEDICARE HOSPITAL STATUS

A Medicare patient admitted into a hospital for 3 consecutive days is eligible for rehabilitation in a nursing home. **Be sure** that the patient has been *admitted* and not labeled *for observation* to the hospital. This one-word difference will make the difference between Medicare or the patient paying for the rehabilitation costs. If this happens: Ask the doctor if they can change the status, ask the hospital ombudsman for assistance, or appeal to Medicare.

Medicare Compare (free)
Medicare Hotline
800-633-4227 or www.medicare.gov

Medicare Rights Center
800-333-4114 or www.medicarerights.org

The National Committee for Quality Assurance
(NCQA) Health Plans Report Cards (free)
reportcards.ncqa.org/#/health-plans/list
List of HMOs and their accreditation status
888-275-7585 or www.ncqa.org

The National Research Corporation
800 388-4264 or www.nationalresearch.com

Your State Health Department or
State Insurance Department

Medicare Prescription Plans

The Medicare Prescription Drug Plan (Plan D) offers optional drug coverage plans that may help lower prescription drug costs. You will pay a monthly premium for your plan. When your out-of-pocket drug costs fall between the range of $3,820 and $5,100 (donut hole), you qualify for a discount. You'll pay 25% of the costs of covered brand-name drugs and 44% of the costs of covered generic drugs.

Check if your income meets the level where you will pay an income-related monthly adjustment in addition to the premium. This will be deducted from your monthly Social Security benefit payment; if the amount is more than your payment, you will receive a bill.

You can enroll each year during the period from October 15 through December 7, with coverage to begin on January 1 of the following year. Each year during this period, even if you are satisfied with your plan, review your choices. Plans can change costs and benefits. Verify that your medications are still covered. When turning 65, you can enroll during the period three months before and after the month of your 65th birthday. If you do not select a Medicare prescription drug plan when you are first eligible and do not have other prescription

drug coverage at least as good (called creditable coverage) as Medicare, you may have to pay an ongoing penalty if you select a plan at a later date.

If you or your spouse's employer or union has determined that your current coverage, on average, is at least as good as the Medicare drug coverage (creditable coverage), you can keep your current plan as long as it is still offered. Once the employer or union no longer offers its drug plan, you will not have to pay a penalty as long as you join a Medicare drug plan within 63 days after the coverage ends.

If your Medigap policy covers prescription drugs, you should receive information on how the Medicare prescription drug plans' coverage will affect your Medigap policy. If you have a Medigap policy with prescription drug coverage and keep it and then later choose to join a Medicare prescription drug plan, you will have to pay the ongoing penalty.

If you do not take a lot of prescriptions currently, consider joining a drug plan now and paying the lowest premium.

For more information, check www.medicare.gov/find-a-plan and the National Council on Aging website at www.benefitscheckup.org.

Medicare Advantage

The Medicare Advantage plans, offered by private insurers, provide extra benefits and lower co-payments than original Medicare and also covers the cost for most drugs. Medicare Advantage Plans include Medicare health maintenance organizations (HMO), preferred provider organizations (PPO), private fee-for-service plans and Medicare special-needs plans and can include prescription drug coverage.

However, you may have to see doctors who belong to the plan or go to certain hospitals to get services. Before signing up, make sure your doctor and other providers are in the network.

Medicare Advantage members can switch to traditional Medicare and a Part D drug plan between January 1-March 31. Open enrollment for Medicare Advantage and Part D drug plans will run from October 15 to December 7. To join a Medicare Advantage plan, you must have

Medicare Part A and Part B. You will have to pay your monthly Medicare Part B premium to Medicare. In addition, you might have to pay a monthly premium to your Medicare Advantage plan for the extra benefits that they offer. Review your plan carefully for out-of-pocket costs.

If you join a Medicare Advantage plan, your Medigap policy won't work. This means it won't pay any deductibles, co-payments, or other cost-sharing under your Medicare health plan. You have a legal right to keep the Medigap policy. If you move and your plan is based on a regional network, you will have to enroll in a new Medicare Advantage program.

Medicare HMO

It is important to note that there is no standard health maintenance organization (HMO). Plans vary widely in terms of services offered, the quality of those services, and amounts charged.

Some HMOs offer more benefits than traditional Medicare and do so at a lower cost, others are reducing benefits and still others are withdrawing coverage completely in certain areas.

In an HMO, health care providers are banded into a network. You are assigned a **primary care physician** (some plans may use a nurse practitioner working with a physician) who coordinates your health care through this network. The primary care physician takes care of your routine medical needs. To see a specialist, you must first gain the permission of the primary care physician (who in turn may need to gain approval from an HMO administrator).

If you select an HMO, your Medicare Part B premium remains the same. Medicare pays the HMO, on your behalf, a monthly premium that covers both Part A and Part B coverage. It is important to note that Medicare HMOs offer all traditional Medicare benefits (Part A hospital insurance plus Part B medical insurance), usually without deductibles or co-payments. Thus, the need for a Medigap policy is eliminated. But, **don't drop your Medigap policy**; you might want to keep it for a while. You currently can switch from an HMO to fee-for-service Medicare, but you might face problems getting a Medigap policy if

your health has changed. It may be a good idea to continue your Medigap policy for a few months while you experience the services from your HMO.

Medicare HMOs usually offer additional benefits not generally covered by Medicare (preventive care, eye care, prescription drugs, inoculations, etc.). Enrollment in an HMO may provide access to a broader array of health services at an overall lower cost. HMOs are in a period of change; some curtail their service areas and/or reduce their benefits. Check your hospital, your family doctor, and your office on aging. Check for changes in benefits and costs.

How HMOs Work

It is important to understand how an individual HMO is paid by Medicare and, in turn, how it pays its participating physicians.

Some plans put the doctor at risk. They pay the doctor a set amount for each Medicare patient assigned. If the cost of the service is less, the doctor wins; if the cost of the service is higher, the doctor loses. These plans are called capitated plans, because doctors are paid on a per person or per capita basis. Doctors have a financial interest in limiting your access to expensive care. You should exercise caution with plans that pay their participating physicians bonuses for limiting expensive care.

Non-capitated plans pay the provider only when the beneficiary uses services, and a larger co-payment may be required. Generally, better plans pay their health care providers according to the services they provide. If you make a visit, the doctor gets paid; if you don't, the doctor doesn't get paid. This is good because it will motivate the doctor to want to see you (you usually will have to pay a modest co-payment). Some other non-capitated plans simply pay their doctors a salary, which relieves negative financial pressures on their decisions concerning your medical care.

In assessing an HMO, focus on its reputation for promptly providing needed services regardless of the cost involved. An HMO's service ethic is ultimately the most decisive factor in judging its appropriateness for you. **Health care is more than a financial decision**.

HMO Concerns

There are many HMOs nationwide. Some are better than others. The central issues in determining whether an HMO is good include: Are the plan's doctors qualified? Are its affiliated hospitals well-recommended? Will you be able to see your primary care physician without delay? Will you get access to specialist care in a timely manner when you need it?

This last question is particularly crucial since medicine operates in a gray area. It is not always clear that specialist care is needed. The use of specialized care has driven up the cost of health care for all of us. But has a particular HMO gone too far? Does it deny access to reasonable care? The only way to determine this is to ask around. What has been the experience of your friends and neighbors? Talk to doctors inside and outside the plan. Find out what percentage of the HMO's members have dropped their coverage in the past year. If this number is greater than 15%, watch out. In short, before joining an HMO, do your homework.

If you join an HMO, you can switch plans only once a year, between November 15 and December 31. When changing from one HMO to another, do not disenroll from your existing one before first enrolling directly in the new HMO. Once established, you will be automatically disenrolled from the original HMO. Keep in mind that if you want to enroll in traditional fee-for-service insurance, **you may not be automatically eligible for a Medigap policy**.

If you leave your HMO within the first twelve months of initially selecting a Medicare HMO option or if you move out of your health plan's service area, Medigap insurers cannot deny your application. This is the case as long as you remember to apply within 63 days of leaving your HMO. If you have exercised the Medicare HMO option for longer than a year and then decide to switch to traditional Part B Medicare or if you delay in applying, the possibility of obtaining a Medigap policy can be reduced, particularly if you have health problems. It is important to **test your HMO** once you do enroll to be sure it is right for you.

A last concern involving HMOs is that they operate within a defined service area. For most people, this will not be a problem. But for those with children in college, who travel a lot or who regularly take extended vacations away from home, this can be a concern. HMOs are required to cover emergency care costs wherever they occur, but they do not have to pay for routine care outside of their service area. If you expect to spend a lot of time away from home, check with the HMO of your choice to see if they have reciprocal care arrangements with an HMO in the area in which you will be spending substantial time. If you remain in the service area, traditional Medicare fee-for-service or one of the new Medicare Advantage options may be better for you. If you now have Medicare, you can keep your present coverage. Most people do.

Health Savings Accounts

Health savings accounts (HSAs) allow people before they qualify for Medicare to deposit pretax dollars for health expenses and to receive a tax deduction for contributions. The maximum annual contribution for an individual is $3,500 and for a family is $7,000. A catch-up contribution of $1,000 is allowed for those 55 or older. Withdrawals made for qualifying health costs are tax-free. If you can, put in the maximum, since HSAs are portable and unused funds are rolled over and allowed to accumulate from year to year. The account can earn interest and grow tax-free.

To open an HSA, you must buy a high-deductible health insurance policy, and the coverage must be your only health insurance (you may also have long-term care, dental, disability and vision plans). You can withdraw money tax-free to pay for qualified medical expenses until the high deductible is reached. Qualified expenses include co-payments, prescription drugs, doctors' services and long-term care insurance. Non-qualified withdrawals are taxable, and prior to age 65 there is a 20% penalty. Designate a beneficiary for your HSA.

Make sure you save all your related receipts in case you are ever audited. Similar to a tax audit, you will need proof of what you purchased using your account.

Once you are age 65 or go on Medicare, you can no longer contribute to an HSA. If your spouse is the designated beneficiary, your spouse can take over the HSA. If someone other than your spouse is the beneficiary, the account ceases to function as an HSA after your death.

Medicaid

Medicaid is a program of assistance to those of any age who need medical services they cannot afford.

There are income and net worth limits for Medicaid eligibility, which differ from state to state. Essentially, a Medicaid recipient and spouse may have income up to a certain amount and also retain assets up to a certain amount, including one's home, and be eligible for Medicaid. Medicaid rules are very complicated. Check with your attorney, senior center, or local government office of aging for specific details. **Check now** so you're prepared when and if you need Medicaid in the future.

Because Medicare does not cover long-term nursing home custodial care, which can be quite costly, Medicaid is often the only option for those who find they need such care.

It is important to keep in mind that you are not expected to exhaust your life savings, go into debt, or sell your home before receiving Medicaid. A lien may be placed on your home to reimburse the state for your expenses.

ACA, or Obamacare

The Affordable Care Act (ACA), or Obamacare, may no longer have a required mandate. Please check. There may be other possible changes to ACA.

Under ACA, each state has its own marketplace (exchange); many marketplaces are run by the federal government. Insurers and premiums will vary in each state (see www.healthcare.gov). Before signing up for a policy, make sure your doctors, hospitals and other providers are covered in the plan. Going outside the plan can be expensive. Under ACA, it is possible for your family to have separate providers of insurance. Be aware that if you received a premium subsidy and your income rose during the year, you could owe a tax bill.

In 2019, the federal individual mandate fee no longer applies. But some states passed individual mandates that require residents to have health insurance or pay a state tax penalty.

If you currently have a policy, you will automatically be reenrolled in your current plan unless you take action. This could cost money. The premiums charged by your current account could increase, and new plans may be available. Review the plans during the open enrollment period, from November 1 through December 15. Check since there may be changes to ACA.

You can still buy coverage directly from insurers outside the marketplace. They may have lower premiums. Private exchanges are separate and distinct from ACA. You can buy private insurance from a health insurance agent. See eHealthInsurance.com.

Retirees enrolled in Medicare are not eligible for marketplace coverage. As you near age 65 and are enrolling in Medicare, don't forget to notify your marketplace plan that you will be dropping coverage. Coordinate the end date of your plan with the effective date of your Medicare enrollment. Keeping your marketplace plan may be a mistake since you will no longer be eligible for any tax credits that offset the marketplace plan's costs. There may be changes to this program, so check HealthCare.gov.

Long-Term Care Insurance

Neither Medicare nor Medigap nor HMOs will cover non-medical at-home care or the full costs of nursing home expenses. It is estimated that 69% of people will need some type of long-term care. The average nursing home costs $90,520 per year and can be considerably more in certain areas. There are long-term care policies that help protect assets that otherwise might have to be liquidated in order to pay the high costs of nursing home care. Experts seem to agree that you should consider buying a long-term care policy at age 50. Obtain a policy with a minimum coverage of 5 years, a protection against inflation, and a deductible of 20 to 30 days. Make sure your policy covers an option for home care benefits that include payment to family members who assist in care and will cover the cost of nursing homes and assisted living facilities. Ask if the home care provider could be hired through a licensed agency or an individual provider, which could be less expensive.

Some states allow state income deduction or credit for premiums. These vary from state to state. Long-term care premiums can now be paid through sheltered HSAs, and these HSAs are 100% tax-deductible, are portable and can be withdrawn at age 65 without penalty, or they can be saved like a retirement plan.

Be sure to purchase a policy that does not raise the premium as you grow older. Be careful: The policies are very complicated. Don't be pressured into buying one. For you, it might not be a good deal.

LONG-TERM CARE INFO

U.S. Dept. of Health & Human Services
Longtermcare.gov

Free publication:
**A Shopper's Guide to
Long-Term Care Insurance**
1100 Walnut Street, Suite 1500
Kansas City, MO 64106-2197
816-783-8300 • www.naic.org
Link to guide: naic.org/documents
/prod_serv_consumer_ltc_lp.pdf

Health Records

Maintain your own medical records by writing down relevant facts about your health, your test results, and a list of current medications, dosages and supplements. List any symptoms you may be experiencing. Keep a copy of your living will (see Chapter 4). Collect as much information as you can about the health history of your family, and share it with your doctor. The U.S. Surgeon General's Family History Initiative aims to raise public awareness of the importance of knowing your family health history. To access the free software, go to http://familyhistory.hhs.gov. You can then document your family's health history.

Steps for an Appeal

Have you been denied a claim for a service you received? If so, you have the right to appeal. Depending on the type of coverage you have, the appeal process will vary. Steps to take:

- **Document everything**. As you proceed, keep records of all interactions with your provider, doctor or hospital. Document every call, conversation or e-mail. Note the name, date, time and what you talked about. Keep a copy of all documents that you send.

- If your medical condition requires prompt attention, pay the bill under protest. Then proceed with your appeal.

- Thousands appeal every year. Appellants win approximately 35% of the time, but it takes tenacity.

- Be strong but civil. Even though you may be upset, you can get your point across better by being courteous and rational.

- For assistance, contact your local State Health Insurance Assistance Program (SHIP) at www.shiptacenter.org or 877-839-2675 or hire a medical advocate. Search by state, and find one that is association-certified.

Medicare Appeal

- Check www.medicare.gov/appeals to see: How Do I File an Appeal?

- Get the Medicare Summary Notice (MSN). Highlight the item you are appealing.

- Ask your doctor to support your appeal.

- Write an explanation of why you disagree with the decision.

- Be sure that all of your personal information on the notice is accurate: name, Medicare claim number and phone number.

- Make a copy of the notice and your explanation, and keep it for your records.

- Send your appeal to the company that handles the billing.

- You must file your appeal within 120 days of the date you get the MSN in the mail. You should get a decision within 60 days.

- If your appeal is turned down, you have 180 days to ask for a rehearing. Submit any additional information at this time. You should get a decision within 60 days.

- If your appeal is rejected again, you have 60 days to request a hearing with an administrative law judge for a fee.

Medicare Advantage Appeal

Medicare Advantage is usually an in-network plan. If you go out of network or fail to get preauthorization for a procedure, you will get billed. Know the rules for your coverage, and keep notes of authorizations, specialist referrals and other relevant information.

The appeals can vary from plan to plan.

- You must file your appeal within 60 days from receiving written notification of the denial.

- Write an explanation of why you disagree with the decision, requesting a redetermination.

- For a payment request, the plan has 60 days to respond. For a standard service request, the plan has 30 days to respond.

- If an expedited decision is required, your doctor should make the request. The plan should answer within 72 hours of receipt.

- If your appeal is turned down, the plan must submit its decision to an independent agency for review.

- If your appeal is rejected again, you can request a hearing with an administrative law judge for a fee.

- Review your Medicare Advantage plan's communications for detailed information about their processes and time lines.

Medicare Prescription Drug Appeal

The appeals process can vary from plan to plan.

- You must file your appeal within 60 days from receiving written notification of the denial.

- Write an explanation of why you disagree with the decision, requesting a redetermination. Some plans allow phone or e-mail requests.

- You should get a decision within 72 hours; if it is an expedited decision, the plan must respond within 24 hours.

- If your appeal is turned down, once you resubmit your appeal, the plan has 7 days to respond. For an expedited request, the plan must respond ASAP but no later than 72 hours.

- If your appeal is rejected again, you can request a hearing with an administrative law judge for a fee.

REVIEW EMPLOYER'S POLICY

When you are planning to retire, review your employer's policy on health insurance. Once you retire, will your employer: continue coverage, ask you to contribute for coverage, cover your spouse and family? **Make sure you and your family are not left unprotected.**

"It takes hands to build a house, but only hearts can build a home."

—*Author Unknown*

Where Will You Live?

Where shall we live when we're retired?
Should we move or stay here?
If we move, where should we go?

Those are probably the most discussed questions when families begin looking ahead to settling down into retirement life. They are very serious questions. The right decision could determine how comfortable, happy and secure retirement will be.

Americans are very mobile. Moving is a way of life because of job changes and transfers. In a study by Age Wave, nearly two-thirds of retirees have either moved or plan to move within the same community or into homes in other cities and states.

The wide separation of families and friends is in sharp contrast to well-rooted, close-knit families and communities abroad. Perhaps seeking to restart ties, as retirement approaches, many Americans consider moving closer to children, grandchildren, other relatives or good friends who have moved away.

But should you? There are many factors to be considered in addition to a natural desire to be closer to family and friends. It's not enough to say, "It would be good to be nearer the kids."

Their way of life may not be yours. Their friends might not become your friends. If they should decide to seek better job opportunities elsewhere, you might be left behind, lonelier than ever.

Start thinking early about where you would be happiest in retirement. Remember: Where you live in retirement will be a critical factor in what you do for the extra income you might need, for personal relationships, for leisure activities, for health and comfort, etc. Explore all your options.

It is not too early to think about all of this, even if retirement is still 10 years in the future. There are a number of options available. What you choose will depend upon your own circumstances, needs and preferences. Your health may dictate that you should move to a milder climate. Your plans for leisure activities may make you move closer to nature or keep you close to the cultural offerings of a larger city or college town.

Moving Is Appealing, but...

The majority of those retiring say that they have given some thought to relocating. However, most stay where they are.

Studies indicate that only 20% to 25% of those who retire move away from their home communities within the first few years of retirement. Most who move stay in the same state. Perhaps no more than 5% move to other states and other parts of the country.

Of the 75% to 80% who remain in their home communities, a substantial number move to smaller homes or apartments.

Whether you are moving to a smaller home or out of state, this could be the time to downsize some of your belongings, distribute some family treasures to your family members or friends or donate some items to charity.

Most Stay Put

Why do most people stay where they are? It's not simply inertia. Many are too closely tied to homes to move away. They value the memories. They want to remain near friends and neighbors, family and grandchildren, to stay in their clubs and religious organizations with people they know, to do business with banks and stores they are accustomed to and, if they want to continue to work, to stay close to professional contacts. In a nutshell, they want to continue living as much as possible as they did before retirement.

In thinking about where you will live in retirement, it is a good idea to begin by thinking about where you are living now. Why did you choose your present home? What are its advantages? What are its disadvantages?

Did you make sacrifices in order to be convenient to your job or, perhaps, your spouse's job? To be near schools, no longer an advantage now that children are grown? To have space you no longer need, perhaps a larger yard for the children?

Think, also, of what you might gain—or give up—by moving into a smaller home requiring less care, inside and outdoors, and costing less for utilities and perhaps for taxes.

Live With Relatives

Health factors may combine with economic ones to make living with children a necessity. The need for privacy suggests that even in these conditions, measures should be taken to avoid the unnecessary stress that can occur when two independent family units are forced into close association. It will require tact, maturity and considerable caring on the part of family members to survive such forced intimacy without a deterioration of relationships.

There should be an understanding about roles in the family.

Where possible, private living room, bedroom and bath facilities will enable the individual to have an independence that is important to self-respect. Efforts should be made to encourage the family member to maintain a schedule of activities independent of the activities of the family. Interests and friendships should be cultivated apart from the home.

FOR INFORMATION

For information on **home care, assisted living and nursing homes,** see Chapter 15.

Relocation Considerations

Go slow about making a final commitment. Moving is physically and psychologically difficult, and it can be an expensive drain on retirement resources.

Be absolutely sure of whatever decision you make. Here are some things to consider:

- **Climate, geography and scenery:** No place offers a perfect year-round climate. It's a good idea to visit a location you're interested in at different times of the year—and stay long enough to recognize the flaws along with the advantages. Subscribe to the local newspaper; this will give you a sampling of the good and bad news in the area.

Checklist

✔ *for Living*

Yes	No	
❏	❏	Is my present house suitable for retirement living?
❏	❏	Can my present house be remodeled for satisfactory retirement living?
❏	❏	Will I be able to handle the upkeep and maintenance of the house?
❏	❏	Will the costs of taxes and insurance be in my budget?
❏	❏	Can my house be converted to a two-family house to rent?
❏	❏	Have I checked the zoning?
❏	❏	Have I considered using my home equity for income?
❏	❏	Is my present neighborhood safe?
❏	❏	Have I checked the security of my house?
❏	❏	Have I planned how to spend my time?
❏	❏	Am I active in my community?
❏	❏	Are my friends important to me?
❏	❏	Is it important to be near my family?
❏	❏	Do I want to keep working after I retire?
❏	❏	Do I want to stay where I'm known?
❏	❏	Do I want to make a fresh start somewhere else?
❏	❏	Before I move to a new area, have I experienced its different seasons?
❏	❏	Is it close to shopping and public transportation?
❏	❏	Is it near good medical care?

Be very careful—Get legal and financial advice.

- **Health advantages and facilities:** Many who relocate do so for health reasons. Respiratory, coronary and rheumatic conditions might be relieved by settling in the right place or can be aggravated by a wrong choice. When making a decision about moving, consult your doctor. And check on the availability of doctors and hospitals or clinics, wherever you go. Don't take for granted that emergency help will be available. Medicare Advantage plans that are based on regional networks don't transfer at all. You'll have to enroll again. Check www.medicare.gov to find a new plan before you move.

- **Economics:** Check the cost of living in any area in which you want to locate. It's a good idea to subscribe to a local newspaper and read it carefully to learn about prices (check the ads) and business activity. If you want to augment your income in retirement, are there job opportunities? Want ads might tell you, but you probably will have to check the Chamber of Commerce or a senior citizen agency. Remember, if you save money on clothing, heating and housing costs in Sun Belt areas, the savings may be partially offset by air conditioning costs during most of the year. Know what the leisure and association fees are. If you are moving to an active-adult community, know all the costs before you buy.

  Before signing, have a lawyer or a geriatric care manager review the community's financial statements, annual report and contract. If you are being guaranteed care at no extra cost or if you run out of money, look at the actuarial analysis; be sure that they have the wherewithal to keep that commitment.

- **Religious and social opportunities:** Make sure that you can continue to enjoy the kind of religious and social life you have had before. Are the facilities available? Generally, they are almost everywhere, but be sure to check. The same advice goes for recreational and sports possibilities and for hobbies. The friendship you find in religious, social, recreational, sports and hobby groups is important to your happiness in a new home.

- **Cultural and intellectual advantages:** Communities that are desirable places to live may be limited in cultural and intellectual opportunities. College towns offer many features: medical facilities, libraries, cultural organizations, concerts, sporting events and art galleries. Many allow retirees to audit classes for free. Many retirees volunteer at a college.

- **Location and accessibility:** Shopping centers, restaurants, libraries, theaters, post offices, and other everyday facilities you might want are easily accessible almost everywhere now. Certainly you'll have no problems if you have a car. Still, check. Also, don't forget to look into the accessibility of airports offering adequate flight service. Is there train and bus service?

- **Personal relationships:** If you have no friends or relatives in the place you'd like to make your retirement home, visit enough times to be sure the residents are congenial. Almost always they will be, but outsiders may find it hard to break through barriers in a few places. The lack of quick friendliness and total acceptance in a community creates additional strain at a time when tearing up roots in one place and trying to set them in another is traumatic enough.

KEEP UP TO DATE

- **Legal considerations:** If you move out of state, you should have your will reviewed and possibly a new will drawn up in your new home state, since laws can differ from state to state. If you are going to live in two states, check that your will, power of attorney and health care proxy follow both states rules.

When you consider moving, decide what you want and need in a new home. Check carefully rather than deciding on a basis of community ads or sunshine when you've just left winter snow. Visit at different times of the year. Summer vacations could be a start, but take time to sample other seasons. Being cautious may prevent you from being sorry when it's too late.

There is a good test of how happy and well adjusted a retiree will be in a new retirement home.

How happy are you in your present community?

If you are happy and active in your area and enjoying its advantages and helping to serve its needs, there is almost no doubt that you can be as happy and adjusted in your new home.

If you have never become a part of your neighborhood, because you are too busy and just not interested, don't expect changes if you relocate.

When you go into a new community, don't wait to be invited to church, service or other clubs or to participate in activities generally. Introduce yourself, mention what you were interested in before and say, "I'd like to be a part of things here."

If you decide to relocate, the success of your move in the long run will be up to you.

Moving Concerns

If you are moving with a moving company, be wary. Get at least three quotes in writing; the movers should come to your home to evaluate your belongings. Get references from friends who have actually used the moving company. Check to see if they are part of the American Moving and Storage Association, www.moving.org, and ask for their U.S. Department of Transportation (DOT) number to see if they are registered.

If you experience trouble, you can file a complaint with the DOT's Federal Motor Carrier Safety Administration at 888-368-7238 or fmcsa.dot.gov/contact-us. Check these websites for tips, suggestions and consumer complaints: www.movingscam.com and www.protectyourmove.gov. There are federal guidelines on how to weigh shipments but not on measuring volume, so be very wary of movers that charge by the cubic foot. Check if your homeowner's insurance covers your belongings while in transit.

When you move, secure important documents like medical records, power of attorney, birth certificates, and Social Security cards, and keep them with you.

Taxes

There are many programs that give senior or disabled homeowners a break.

States are often adjusting their tax systems. If moving to another state, county or municipality, find out what your total tax burden will be. Review all income taxes, sales taxes, property taxes, and estate and inheritance taxes. Some states will charge income tax on Social Security and pension benefits. For more information:

- Retirement Living Information Center, www.retirementliving.com; see Taxes by State
- Kiplinger's State-by-State Guide to Taxes on Retirees, www.Kiplinger.com/links /retireetaxmap

---

TAXES AND THE SALE OF YOUR HOME

When you sell your primary residence, you can deduct up to $250,000 in profit if you're single, $500,000 if you're married. The exclusion can be used more than once. The home or apartment must be the primary residence of at least one spouse for at least two of the past five years. A surviving spouse can sell a home that was jointly owned within 2 years of the spouses passing away and still file for the $500,000 capital-gains exclusion. If you sell your primary home, be aware that high profit sales can trigger the special 3.8% Medicare tax, which will be assessed only if the seller has an adjusted gross income of $200,000 for singles and $250,000 for couples. On sales of second homes, the Medicare tax can hit the entire gain.

Checklist ✓ *for Safety*

Yes	No	
❏	❏	Do you have no-slip tape in your bathtub or shower?
❏	❏	Do you have grab bars and hand grips in showers and bathtubs and near toilets?
❏	❏	Can your towel bars and soap holders withstand sudden pulls?
❏	❏	Do you keep throw rugs away from the tops and bottoms of stairs?
❏	❏	Do all rugs have no-slip mats under them?
❏	❏	Do you wear loose-fitting slippers or bathrobes?
❏	❏	Are all chairs and stairs sturdy and free of wobbles?
❏	❏	Have you replaced all frayed cords and broken plugs?
❏	❏	Have you relocated all furniture, lamp cords and clutter from traffic paths?
❏	❏	Do you avoid running extension cords under rugs or carpets?
❏	❏	Do you avoid using space heaters, if possible? If they are necessary, are they away from flammable materials and out of traffic lanes?
❏	❏	Do you make sure you do not smoke while lying down?
❏	❏	Have you installed smoke, heat, and carbon monoxide detectors throughout the house?
❏	❏	Have you installed fire extinguishers near the kitchen and work room?
❏	❏	Do you have escape routes planned from all areas of home in case of fire?
❏	❏	Do you avoid overloading one socket with several plugs?
❏	❏	Have you discarded heavy, hard-to-handle, or broken cooking utensils?
❏	❏	Are there handrails on all stairs and inclines?
❏	❏	Have you installed night-lights in the bedroom, bathroom and hallways?
❏	❏	Have you made sure stairways and other areas are well lighted?
❏	❏	Do you have a flashlight by the bed?
❏	❏	If you live alone, do you have a friend or relative check in with you at regular intervals?
❏	❏	Do you keep a first-aid kit handy? Did you take a first-aid course or CPR course? Do you have emergency phone numbers near your phone?

"Growing old is no more than a bad habit which a busy man has no time to learn."

—*Andre Maurois*

"Don't simply retire from something; have something to retire to."

—*Harry Emerson Fosdick*

"The brain is a wonderful organ. It starts working the moment you get up in the morning and does not stop until you get into the office."

—*Robert Frost*

Earn Money in Retirement

Do you have to work after retirement? Many people who could answer "no" to this question from a purely economic point of view would have to say "yes" from a psychological one. There are other compulsions than not having enough income to live comfortably. Some people work because of the additional rewards that work affords. Some work to have an identity. A recent survey from Golden Gateway Financial shows that, due to concerns about the economy, the retirement age is rising. Now only 40% of seniors plan to retire by age 70.

Americans are living longer and healthier lives. Many retirees prefer a combination of work and leisure to fill their needs. (To work and receive Social Security, see Chapter 3.)

Must I? May I?

The question for many is decided in terms of economic necessity. Work is essential for adequate income. The other question is: Given that I wish to work, will I be able to find a job? Who will be interested in having an individual who has been retired from active work? How can I compete with younger worker in terms of strength, ability to learn, and contribution to the company?

Given a choice, most older workers would prefer continuing with some kind of employment. Work makes a contribution to our lives that is not easily replaced by anything else. What, other than work, can give the following satisfactions to life?

- It is the basis for self-respect and the feeling that you have something to contribute.

- It is a source of prestige and recognition. People appreciate your ability to perform.

- It provides a place for social participation. Many friendships are related to the job.

- It is a source of enjoyment, a chance to be creative.

- It is a way of helping others.

- It helps give order to the day, making time pass. You don't have to plan for or organize a great part of the day.

- It helps financially: to pay the bills, enjoy a dinner out or take a vacation.

The Enemy Is Us

The greatest obstacle to finding employment may be the attitude that you have about yourself. It's true that there are a number of misconceptions about older workers. But there are some strengths that mature workers have. Focus on the positive things that you have to offer.

The Department of Labor and other agencies have studied the performance of older workers and have come up with the following facts that refute the myths about them:

Myth: "Older workers are too slow. They can't meet production requirements."

Fact: There is no significant drop in performance and productivity. In fact, many older workers exceed the average output of younger employees.

Myth: "Older workers can't meet the physical demands of jobs."

Fact: Few jobs require great strength or heavy lifting. Labor-saving equipment makes it possible to handle jobs without difficulty.

Myth: "Older workers are absent too often."

Fact: The attendance of workers over 65 compares favorably with other age groups.

Myth: "Older workers are inflexible. They're hard to train because they can't accept change."

Fact: Adaptability depends on the individual, not on age. Some young people are set in their ways, while a high proportion of older workers show flexibility in accepting a change in occupation and earnings.

Myth: "Hiring older workers increases our pension and insurance costs."

Fact: Most pension plans provide for benefits related to length of service, earnings, or both. Small, additional pensions, when incurred, are more than offset by the worker's experience, lower turnover, and quality of work. The costs of group life, accident, and health insurance and workers' compensation are *not* materially increased by hiring older workers.

Which favorable or unfavorable attitudes toward older workers apply to you?

- Defeatist attitude toward getting work and difficult time impressing an employer favorably.

- Stability that comes with maturity.

- Wastes less time on job than younger worker.

- You feel like you are slowing down, and talk about this feeling with a prospective employer.

- Forgotten how to go about getting a job.

- Less absenteeism; more apt to stay on the job.

- Safe work habits.

- Reluctant to change occupations even if there is no work available in line with previous work.

- Refuses to consider jobs paying less or having less prestige than former jobs because of personal pride.

- Difficulty making a realistic evaluation of limitations. Makes unrealistic demands as to wages, location, working conditions, etc.

- Greater sense of responsibility.

- Steady work habits and serious attitude.

- Good appearance.

- Requires less supervision, once trained.

- Tends to undersell self and fails to impress prospective employers favorably.

- Less distracted by outside interests, has fewer domestic troubles, and is capable of greater concentration.

If You Had Your Druthers...

Match your interests, skills, experiences and situation while looking for a job. You need to look at all of these factors to get a total picture. You may be interested in doing something for which you have little experience. You may not like the kind of work in which you have experience. Try brainstorming with your answers to the following questions:

WHY WORK IN RETIREMENT?

A survey of 60- to 70-year-olds:

To keep mentally active	64%
To keep physically active	54%
To keep connected with others	43%
To make money	41%
A sense of self worth	34%
New challenges	33%
Health insurance	23%

Source: Merrill Lynch and HSBC

Past Jobs Held
What did you like and dislike?

Skills and Abilities
What can you do best?

Educational Qualifications
Have you had special instruction?

Physical Limitations
Does your health rule out some jobs?

Goals
What would be ideal for you?

Your Resume

The resumé is the tool for you to get the interview. Be sure your resumé is clear and understandable. Highlight your experience. Start with your accomplishments, focus on ways you excelled, and show your skills and how you can contribute to the company. Use keywords; many companies digitize resumés, searching for keywords. Never lie, don't exaggerate and stay honest.

Legally, employers cannot ask how old you are but, from your resumé, they can guess. Leave the

Your Experience Inventory

Employment Objective (As clearly and concisely as possible, indicate what you want to do)

_____

_____

Employment History (List employment in reverse chronological order)

Dates: From–To	Job Title & Responsibilities	Company Name & Location
_____	_____	_____
_____	_____	_____
_____	_____	_____

Miscellaneous Employment (List part-time and/or minor employments, if these would help)

_____

_____

Education (List schools in reverse chronological order)

Dates: From–To	Name of School & Location	Degree/Last Grade Completed
_____	_____	_____
_____	_____	_____

Additional Education (List correspondence schools, company courses, seminars, etc.)

_____

_____

Professional Associations (List organizations to which you belong or did belong)

_____

_____

Interests (List volunteer activities and hobbies, especially if they relate to the job you want)

_____

_____

year you graduated off your resumé. Be careful what dates you include. For early positions, list a category called Prior Positions Held and leave out dates. If e-mailing a resumé, send it in the body of the e-mail since it could get caught in e-mail spam or they may be unable to open the attachment.

The Job Interview

Be prepared before you arrive for the interview. Research the industry so you can tailor your skills to their needs. In the job interview, you have a few minutes to tell about your qualifications. Start with one or two sentences about where you last worked, what you were good at, and why you're qualified. The key is to define yourself in a way that fits the position. You will likely be talking to someone younger than yourself. The job may pay less than what you earned before retirement. Be confident about yourself to avoid feeling defensive. Discuss your skills and experience realistically.

To leave a favorable impression at your interview:

- Stress your skills, not your limitations.
- Be poised and confident, but not cocky.
- Be pleasant, but business-like.
- Speak firmly and clearly.
- Listen attentively to your interviewer's questions.
- Answer briefly and honestly.
- Stress your stability and good attendance record.
- Ask intelligent questions about the job.
- Be realistic about your salary requirements.

- Leave when the interview is over, thanking the employer for the opportunity.
- Research the company, and read the company's website.
- Practice interviewing with a friend.
- Bring copies of your resumé, and tailor it to the job application.
- Show the interviewer that you are interested in the job.
- If asked about a difficult moment, describe how you solved the problem.
- Stress your skills, i.e., problem solving, interpersonal communications, reading comprehension, customer skills and basic computer skills.
- Write a handwritten thank-you note after the interview.

Do not get dejected if you do not receive the job; many may have applied. Thank the interviewer, and ask them to keep you in mind for future job opportunities.

How Not to Impress

Poor impressions are left by those who…

- Are timid and ill at ease.
- Are stubborn and argumentative.
- Stress their need for a job.
- Emphasize their age or personal problems.

- Exaggerate their skills.
- Criticize a former employer.
- Talk too long.
- Discuss salary, benefits, and hours before the employer brings up the subjects.
- Show reluctance to fill out an application, give references or take a physical exam.

Job Search Sources

There are sources of help in locating a job or developing the skills needed to get one. They are:

- Friends, relatives, former co-workers, or members of your social group. Tell them that you're looking for a job, and ask them for help in finding one.
- Want ads in newspapers, professional journals, and trade magazines.
- Company websites.
- Industrial and craft unions.
- Private employment agencies (some charge a fee).
- Yellow pages of telephone directory, industrial directories and Chamber of Commerce lists.
- Professional associations.
- Online job sites like www.LinkedIn.com, www.workforce50.com, www.monster.com, www.Military.com/veteran-jobs, www.Retiredbrains.com, Indeed.com, Coolworks.com, and www.retirementjobs.com.
- Temporary agencies. Many temporary jobs lead to permanent positions.
- Forty-Plus Clubs for executives in major cities.

- Military Officers Association of America (for members). 201 N. Washington St., Alexandria, VA 22314-2539, 800-234-6622, www.moaa.org
- Personnel offices.
- College placement offices.
- The library.
- Nonprofit employment agencies. Your local Chamber of Commerce, the Y, Salvation Army, and state employment agency should be able to tell you if there are agencies in your area.

BE CAREFUL about putting your resumé online; it could be the start of identity theft. Use job sites that allow you to hide your contact information and where an employer must click on a link to e-mail you. If you must make your information public, use your first initial, omit your street address and phone number, and set up a temporary e-mail address. **Do not give out your Social Security number** until you verify that the recruiter and position are for real.

Second Careers

In today's job market, with early retirement and company mergers, many find themselves looking for a new job or a new career at a relatively early age. This is a marked change from the employment stability many enjoyed ten and twenty years ago. Millions of Americans have been and will be affected by this change.

What to do? While still working, continually develop your skills—at work or at your local adult educational center, community college, or university. Take courses that interest you and in subject areas where job possibilities could develop. Volunteering can open possibilities; some employers pick employees from their volunteer groups.

What a Worker in 2019 Nets From a Job			
Employment Income (Annual)	**$30,000.00**	**$40,000.00**	**$50,000.00**
Social Security tax (FICA)	2,295.00	3,060.00	3,825.00
Additional federal/state taxes (estimated)	4,500.00	6,000.00	7,500.00
Job expenses (travel, lunch, etc.) (estimated)	3,000.00	3,000.00	3,000.00
Net Earnings	**20,205.00**	**27,940.00**	**35,675.00**
Monthly (Net) Earnings	**1,683.75**	**2,328.33**	**2,972.92**

There are positive factors. You have work skills and experience that are needed almost everywhere.

- Take an inventory of your talents.

- List your goals, what you've always wanted to do and what you would enjoy doing.

- Where are your skills needed?

Work for Yourself—Or Others

If you want to have a good job interview with a person you really like and have your resumé read by admiring and sympathetic eyes, try making an application to *yourself* for a job! You can work out hours that are agreeable to employer and employee. Some retired persons will want to consider being their own boss, and there are many ways this can be done.

Working for Yourself

Operating a part-time business may be your answer to the need to supplement your income and find meaningful ways to invest your time. If it is done on a small scale, it may not require as much capital and know-how as you would imagine.

Considerable caution should be exercised, however, in the selection of a business. On average, your chances of remaining three years in your business are about 50-50. A Dun and Bradstreet survey revealed that 90% of such business failures were due to inexperience. This is the age of the chain store and the corporation. Your choice of a business should not lead you into competition with such tough competitors.

Check a regional office of the Small Business Administration for advice and information about opening a business at www.sba.gov, or write to:

United States Small Business Administration District Office, 409 3rd Street, SW, Washington, DC 20416 800-827-5722

Try to get an early start preparing for the business you will operate in retirement. You will need time to familiarize yourself with the business, accumulate the capital needed for the investment, and purchase equipment needed *before* attempting

THE BUSINESS PLAN: ITS USES

If you wish to start your own business, preparing a good business plan is the first step. If you need financing or want to bring your bank manager on board in case you run into problems, you'll need a business plan. Having a thorough one demonstrates that you are a self-starter who has put a great deal of thought into your business idea.

Aside from money matters, a business plan will help your overall management of your new enterprise. Getting the business plan right can mean the difference between success and failure.

What does a good business plan look like? Each business plan is different but, in general, it should include a description of the business, including short- and long-term goals, an analysis of the market being entered (including a discussion of competitors' strengths and weaknesses and your competitive advantage), and financial details including start-up costs, the size of the investment required and profit and cash-flow projections for a minimum of one year ahead.

to live on a retirement budget. You must do some research. Find out who needs your product or service and who you will compete with.

Most importantly, you must develop a business plan. Contact SCORE, an organization that can help entrepreneurs find mentors, at 800-634-0245 or www.score.org. It works in partnership with the U.S. Small Business Administration.

The highest rate of entrepreneurship is between the ages of 55–64. Those who use their life experiences have a greater chance of success.

Choosing Your Business

Answering the questions listed below should give you some insights into the type of business that best suits you.

- How well do I get along with other people?

- Am I ready to assume responsibility for payroll and business obligations?

- Am I a good organizer?
- Do I like the proposed business enough to sacrifice for it?
- Am I prepared to take the risk involved in owning a business?
- Do I like to sell?
- Can I make decisions and live with them?
- How do I react to emergencies?

The U.S. Small Business Administration lists 10 characteristics that businesspeople should have.

Rank yourself by 1 (exceptional), 2 (above average), 3 (average), 4 (below average) or 5 (deficient) to find your business potential.

Trait	Rank
Initiative	_____
Positive attitude	_____
Leadership ability	_____
Organizing ability	_____
Industry	_____
Responsibility	_____
Quick and accurate judgments	_____
Sincerity	_____
Perseverance	_____
High level of energy	_____

The more "1s" and "2s" you have listed, the easier it will be for you to adjust to running a business.

Considering the high mortality rate of business and the possibilities of over-extending yourself in demands on your money, health and time, get plenty of information, and be sure that you know what you need before going into business.

Working at Home

Having your business where you live—more than 40 million Americans work out of their homes—eliminates some of the problems of working at a separate location. You do not have to worry about paying rent for the business, nor do you have to incur transportation costs getting to and from work.

It will also be easier to maintain a schedule that is more relaxed if you are working out of your own home.

One warning, though: Check out any zoning regulations or licensing procedures that you might have to comply with as far as businesses in private homes. Be sure you're covered by adequate insurance.

Franchises

This is the kind of business venture that has some of the features of owning your own business and some of the features of working for somebody else. You have to put up some capital, but often the national organization has standards and methods of operation that are part of your obligation to the jointly owned business. The organization often will assume responsibility for giving you training and will supervise the market so that no unfair competition will arise from another member of the same organization.

Franchises are really a form of licensing. The franchisor, which is usually an owner of a service, product or method, distributes through affiliated

WHEN CONSIDERING A SECOND CAREER...

| 1–KNOW WHAT YOU WANT FROM YOUR NEW CAREER | 2–TAKE INVENTORY OF YOUR TALENTS AND DREAMS | 3–ENJOY EXPLORING 2nd CAREER OPTIONS | 4–LEARN A NEW CAREER, JOB OR SKILL | 5–HOW ABOUT STARTING YOUR OWN BUSINESS |

dealers who are the franchises. If you purchase a franchise, often you will be given exclusive rights to the area served by your franchise. But you can still run into trouble from other companies offering similar franchises, so be careful to check beforehand for competition in your area.

A franchise should be carefully investigated before the decision is made to invest in it. Many fraudulent promoters are at work in the field, offering schemes that are little more than obligations on the part of the victims to purchase supplies or goods from the promoters.

Good advice is available from Better Business Bureaus, Chambers of Commerce and others so that no individual need stumble into a venture without adequate information.

Working for Others

Look at Chapter 11, on volunteering, to share your time with others. There are jobs that are directly related to service for others, and the compensation is a combination of a modest paycheck and the knowledge that you have made life more rewarding for someone else. These jobs take as much of your time as you care to give.

Be Prepared

If you are seriously interested in developing the skills necessary to go back to work or start your own business, two of the best places to go for information and help are your public library and your local college.

Library shelves usually have sections on employment and retirement; either category might have the facts and advice you're looking for.

Colleges, particularly community colleges, also provide services for job seekers. In addition to courses that can develop skills and expertise in specific areas (such as business, accounting or education), many colleges offer classes designed for adults who wish to know more about developing second careers and getting back into the employment mainstream. Check with your local two-year college for program details.

Books That Can Help

What Color Is Your Parachute? 2019: A Practical Manual for Job-Hunters and Career-Changers. Richard N. Bolles. Ten Speed Press. 2018. ISBN 978-0399581687. $19.99.

Before and After Resumes: How to Turn a Good Resume Into a Great One. Tracy Burns-Martin. Adams Media. 2012. ISBN 978-1440525070. $17.95.

Don't Retire, REWIRE! Third Edition. Jeri Sedlar and Rick Miners. Alpha Books. 2018. $19.99.

"A perpetual holiday is a good working definition of hell."
—*George Bernard Shaw*

"When preparing to travel, lay out all your clothes and all your money. Then take half the clothes and twice the money."

—*Susan Heller*

Leisure Time

- Will your leisure be the perpetual holiday mentioned by Shaw or the time when you discover how to enjoy life as never before?

- Will your use of leisure time result in success or failure in your attempt to achieve happiness during retirement?

- How much leisure time will you have on your hands, and how difficult will your schedule be after full-time employment is no longer the major part of your daytime activities? What will replace the satisfaction that work has afforded?

Answering the above questions will lead you into an examination of yourself: who you really are,

what you really want, what your attitude is toward the use of your time. This chapter will provide you with an opportunity to look at yourself and to consider the alternatives available for structuring your time.

You'll explore what adjustments may be necessary to meet your basic needs as you attempt to fill your life with meaning that is not derived specifically from the work ethic.

Retirement should be a transition from toil to leisure. It should see a transfer of the energies you formerly devoted to making a living to the *new business* of living well. In the transition, you will learn to reallocate your time. Avoid making a financial commitment to any leisure activity until you are sure that your interest won't disappear as you devote more time to it.

Vacation: Each Day of the Year

A vacation is a vacation because it comes infrequently, but a vacation every day of the year? That's something else again. Planning how you will spend your time in retirement is just as important as planning how you will spend your money.

Planning will help you to enjoy a diverse range of meaningful and satisfying activities instead of just mindlessly filling up time. Unplanned time leads to boredom, a feeling of guilt, and a sense of frustration. As strange as it may seem, many people prefer to work even when it is not an economic necessity. Remember to build *quality* into your leisure hours.

Can Work Be More Fun?

A recent study at Duke University's Center on Aging revealed that over half of the 200 men surveyed (52%) said they got more satisfaction from *work* than they did from *leisure*. 55% of the 200 women surveyed said they enjoyed working more than they did having free time.

Replace work colleagues with another network, rediscover play, uncover your passion and continue lifelong learning.

Can You Accept Leisure?

You need to decide if you can accept the free time you have earned. To really enjoy leisure, you will have to learn to *not work*. Teach yourself that it is *right* for you to enjoy doing something for the pleasure it brings. Retrain your mind to accept that leisure is not *inactivity* and that non-work activities may be as necessary and *useful* as those for which we formerly received paychecks.

The goal in retirement is not just to fill your time but to fill it in a meaningful way. Acceptable leisure has the following characteristics:

- We do it because we want to.

- We anticipate it and remember it fondly.

- We may do it alone or with others.

- We feel good about it.

- It contributes to others as well as to ourselves.

- We may do it for fun or profit.

Leisure can affect your health and your wealth. We can lose both if our bodies and minds are wasted through inactivity or in useless occupation.

Learn to enjoy leisure. Work if you wish, and be as active in your retirement as you care to be, but accept the fact that it's OK to enjoy many different activities, including the activity of doing nothing.

Adding Spice to Your Life

What you do with your time should be more than being busy. An activity that neglects your personality is like throwing a life buoy to a drowning person; it keeps the head above the water but doesn't really provide a rescue.

Demand that your efforts be rewarded. Those activities that are worth your time should:

- Create excitement.

- Stimulate you and give you renewed zest.

- Be both physically and intellectually stimulating.

Have your spouse consider the same categories—then compare, and see what things you have in common to explore together in retirement!

"HAVE YOU CONSIDERED REPAIRMAN?"

Maintaining or improving your health is an ideal everyday leisure pursuit.

Travel Information

Buy an *America the Beautiful* Senior Pass for $80 at age 62; for the rest of your life, you will be admitted free to all national parks, monuments and recreation areas and receive half off federal user fees for certain facilities and services. www.nps.gov/fees_passes.htm.
Road Scholar sponsors group travel worldwide; 800-454-5768 or www.roadscholar.org.
Gardenvisit.com finds gardens and landscapes that are open for public visits.
The Evergreen Club provides B&B hospitality for those over 50 in private homes for a modest gratuity. www.evergreenclub.com.
Get off the road and check out a train or boating vacation: VacationsByRail.com and Houseboating.org.
Before traveling, make copies of key documents. Take one copy with you, and leave another set at home with a family member or friend. Do not publicize your travel on social-networking sites. Consider buying travel insurance.
While traveling, take hourly walks. If you're seated, stretch your legs and flex your feet and do not cross your legs at the ankles or knees. This will help blood move toward the heart. Drink plenty of fluids but avoid caffeine or alcohol.

You can protect yourself from getting sick by washing your hands with soap and water and/or

Meeting Your Needs Through Leisure Activities

There are some basic needs that remain constant throughout life, and many of these can be met through a wise selection of leisure activities. Look at some of these basic needs, and see how they compare with your present leisure activities. List alongside the corresponding need the activity that you are presently engaged in which makes a contribution to that need. In the right-hand column, list additional activities that you would like to consider in the future to meet that need.

Need	Present Activities	Projected Activities
Recognition		
Entertainment		
Self-expression, creativity		
Participation, belonging		
Adventure, new experience		
Learning		
Security		
Physical fitness		
Contemplation		
Self-growth		
Usefulness		
Income		

alcohol-based sanitizers, keeping hands away from your face and mouth, not sharing utensils or drinking glasses, drinking only bottled water, and checking with your doctor before traveling.

For travel warnings and other information, check the U.S. State Department, http://travel.state.gov. Check the Centers for Disease Control, www.cdc.gov/travel. Give the U.S. government your itinerary at Free Smart Traveler's Enrollment Program (STEP) at https://TravelRegistration.state.gov so someone can contact you and assist you in an emergency.

Before traveling overseas, call your credit card issuer to notify them of your travel plans and find out about foreign conversions, which can be up to 3% on purchases. Sign up for an international phone package to avoid the high roaming charges.

What's Best for You?

If you like an activity, that is one good reason for considering it, but there are other factors to consider.

Some activities that have brought satisfaction to others have been found to have these qualities:

- Basic skills can be mastered readily.
- Real proficiency can come with practice.
- So many facets that it doesn't become tiresome.
- Within your budget.
- Enlarges a skill you already possess.
- Offers opportunity for self-development.
- Provides a change of pace from your routine.
- Can be practiced all year long.
- Represents a blend of several activities.
- Can be pursued in spite of some physical limitations.
- Puts you in touch with other people.
- Provides challenges to improve or grow or become more proficient in an area of interest.

Checklist

✓ *for Possible Leisure Activities*

- ❏ Acting
- ❏ Bicycling
- ❏ Bird Watching
- ❏ Boating
- ❏ Book Club
- ❏ Bowling
- ❏ Camping
- ❏ Charitable Activities
- ❏ Club
- ❏ Collecting
- ❏ Community Projects
- ❏ Cooking
- ❏ Crafts
- ❏ Dancing
- ❏ Enjoying Nature
- ❏ Entertaining
- ❏ Exercising
- ❏ Family Activities
- ❏ Family Outings

- ❏ Fishing
- ❏ Gardening
- ❏ Genealogy
- ❏ Golf
- ❏ Ham Radio
- ❏ Hiking
- ❏ Historical Societies
- ❏ Investing
- ❏ Jogging
- ❏ Kayaking
- ❏ Knitting
- ❏ Learning
- ❏ Little League Coaching
- ❏ Museums/Art Galleries
- ❏ Music
- ❏ Painting
- ❏ Part-Time Work
- ❏ Photography
- ❏ Politics

- ❏ Reading
- ❏ Religion
- ❏ Repairing Things
- ❏ Road Scholar
- ❏ Scout Master
- ❏ Scrapbooking
- ❏ Sewing
- ❏ Sport Events
- ❏ Swimming
- ❏ Take Courses
- ❏ Teaching
- ❏ Television
- ❏ Tennis
- ❏ Time to Be Alone
- ❏ Traveling
- ❏ Volunteering
- ❏ Walking
- ❏ Woodworking
- ❏ Writing

> "We make a living by what we get, but we make a life by what we give."
> — *Winston Churchill*

> "What we do for ourselves dies with us. What we do for others and the world remains and is immortal."
> — *Albert Pine*

> "The more I help others to succeed, the more I succeed."
> — *Ray Kroc, Founder of McDonald's*

Step One: Help Yourself

In the preceding chapter, we looked at the amount of time you are going to have during retirement and suggested some possible uses for it. We suggested that you take a good look at yourself and fill your time with experiences that give you pleasure. Relax, and have a good time.

In this chapter, we ask you to do the same thing. You probably won't be able to find continual happiness thinking only about yourself.

The human spirit is too great to be content seeking the gratification of its own desires. Because of the sheer fun of sharing, many people feel a keen satisfaction in giving a part of themselves to community service activities.

Plan for meaningful uses of the free time you will have in retirement. A lack of planned time can lead to boredom, a feeling of guilt and a sense of frustration. Devote part of your time to that which gives you personal pleasure: spend time with hobbies, sports, self-expression or creativity, the adventures of travel, further education or just the entertainment of watching television, reading and listening to music. You have *earned* the right to enjoy leisure as you want to spend it.

However, for your fullest satisfaction in retirement years, consider spending part of your free time in volunteer work *with* and *for* others. One in every four adults in the United States does some volunteer work each year. Research has shown that volunteering can improve your quality of life; the benefits include higher self-esteem and a greater sense of well-being. A recent study by Britain's Economic & Social Research Council reports that communities with high levels of volunteerism have lower crime as well as the added benefit of improved personal health and happiness. Volunteering supports meaningful relationships, being productive and keeping active. Older adults who volunteer have lower mortality rates than those who don't.

Remember that being involved with people helps keep the mind sharp, and relationships reduce stress and limit the effects of aging. It might not be much, and it might not be for a long time, but volunteer work does involve a sharing of personal time and interests and participation with others toward a common objective.

Service Instead of Salary

You may not have realized the degree to which your sense of personal worth has been related to your job. During your early and middle years you have a definite (at times almost overwhelming) sense of responsibility. You are needed by your family. You contribute to society through your work.

Community service activities now offer you such job-related satisfactions as:

- The comradeship of congenial people.
- A chance for recognition.
- An opportunity to contribute to a useful goal.
- An opportunity to belong to a worthwhile group.

You need to give of yourself *more* than the service organizations need to have your help. The principal beneficiary of your service is you.

The point is, there's a need—often a very serious need—for every man or woman to serve, somewhere, as a volunteer worker. The extent of participation is up to the volunteer. It can be as little as an hour a week. It can be much more. It can be a minimum of personal involvement, with only routine chores, or it can be deeply personal.

Dr. Allen G. Brailey, a Boston physician, noted the vital role that service plays in assuming the place formerly occupied by the job or the family. "Do not retire from work; retire to more congenial work for the Community Fund, for the church or the schools, for the Scouts." Volunteering is a great way to use your skills and get satisfaction by making a difference in your community.

What Sharing Does

If activities are carefully selected, they can make the following contributions, most of which relate to your personal well-being:

- Lessen the shock of disengagement from work.

- Delay senility.

- Stimulate the mind and body, reducing health problems.

- Combat the waste of human resources.

- Enrich the community through volunteer services.

- Create positive experiences.

- Make use of your life-learned skills for pleasure and to help others.

Albert Schweitzer gives us good direction when he says, "Wherever a man turns, he can find someone who needs him. Even if it is a little thing, do something for which you get no pay but the privilege of doing it. For remember, you don't live in a world all your own. Your brothers are here, too."

Choosing the Best Activity

There are so many needs that you can afford to choose among them to find the one that suits what you have to offer. Begin early—even before you retire. This will give you a chance to practice. Some companies encourage employees approaching retirement to devote time *before* actual retirement to community service. This permits a gradual transfer of interest and skills to a service-oriented job as formal employment draws to a close.

Ask yourself the following questions when considering how to invest your time:

- Is it something about which I care deeply?

- Does it require a skill I possess?

- Does it provide association with congenial people?

- Does it require time I am prepared to give?

- Do I enjoy fixing things (if that is required)?

- Do I enjoy creating things (if that is required)?

- Am I good at selling things (if that is required)?

- Does it involve working with people or things? (Which do I prefer?)

"GEORGE SAID HE'D LOVE TO BE A VOLUNTEER...
...BUT THERE'S NOT MUCH DEMAND FOR WHAT HE DOES BEST."

Nationwide, at least four-and-a-half million people age 65 or over are currently engaged in some type of volunteer work. If you are considering sharing your knowledge and experience through volunteer work, you can begin looking in your own neighborhood. Chances are many groups in your area engage volunteer workers or are seeking their help.

Volunteer opportunities:

- Help in after-school programs
- Assist in Salvation Army programs
- Partake in local Y activities
- Help at your religious organization
- Provide transportation to the aged for shopping and visits to the doctor
- Volunteer in nursing homes or hospitals
- Participate in telephone "reassurance service" for elderly
- Participate in "Meals on Wheels" program
- Read books to the sightless or ill
- Be a literacy volunteer
- Help with 4-H programs, city parks, gardens
- Be a Big Brother/Big Sister
- Assist in Little League
- Sponsor Girl or Boy Scout troop
- Volunteer in city library, historical sites
- Assist in building/repairing community playgrounds
- Be a school volunteer
- Cooperate in Friendly Visitors programs
- Assist in a Red Cross program

Your Interests and Skills

Identify the resources that you have. On the following list, check the things that you do well and would like to share.

- Bookkeeping skills
- Caring for children
- Caring for older people
- Carpentry
- Church interests
- Computer skills
- Cooking skills
- Entertaining skills
- Gardening
- Human concern
- Hunting skills
- Knowledge of athletics
- Legal knowledge
- Library skills
- Meeting people
- Nursing training
- Organizing ability
- Photography skills
- Playing a musical instrument
- Political interests
- Selling ideas
- Speaking skills
- Supervisory skills
- Teaching skills
- Visiting skills
- Working with the handicapped
- Writing experience

Volunteering: When to Begin

You do not have to wait for retirement to begin volunteer work. You can start on a limited basis, as time permits, and extend your service in retirement. The important thing is to develop a way of channeling the extra time you will have in retirement.

In addition to making better use of your free time, there are other benefits to be derived from volunteer service. Such work often leads to new friendships and educational, cultural and social activities.

Your new friends and activities are especially important if you have not maintained outside interests during your working years. By starting volunteer work now, you will be going into retirement with an established circle of friends whose interests are similar to your own.

Another plus for volunteer service: It is good work experience. If you are thinking about starting a second career when you retire, volunteer work can provide the background needed to reach your goal. Or if you are considering a certain line of work but have some doubts, volunteer service may be just the way to help you know for sure.

A recent study showed volunteering for one organization raised a person's life expectancy more than volunteering for several.

Where to Volunteer

Many communities have central bureaus acting as clearinghouses for nonprofit agencies in need of volunteer help. Look in the telephone directory under Volunteer, Community Service Council or Extension Service, or call an organization that interests you. Call the national number or the local chapter.

Your local library should also have listings of volunteer opportunities in the area.

Check with the social, civic and religious groups represented in your community. They will have projects and can refer you to additional agencies that would welcome your participation.

There are groups in every community involved in a variety of interests. Many are intergenerational, creating a diverse and interesting atmosphere. These groups vary from local civic associations to organizations within religious communities, political groups, groups interested in a specific health problem, and gardening and historical clubs. Your life experiences are of great value to your local educational institutions, community colleges, libraries and museums.

Visit your senior center. It can be the center from which community service ideas will originate. Many studies show that individuals who are involved in activities live a healthier, longer, happier life.

- The Points of Light Institute
  600 Means St., Ste. 210,
  Atlanta, GA 30318
  404-979-2900, www.pointsoflight.org

- Senior Corps
  www.seniorcorps.org

- Volunteers of America
  www.voa.org

- The Peace Corps
  855-855-1961, www.peacecorps.gov

- NECS National Executive Service Corps
  1177 Avenue of the Americas, Fifth Floor,
  New York, NY 10036
  212-269-1234 ext. 116, www.nesc.org

- Volunteer Match
  415-241-6868, www.volunteermatch.org

- National Park Service
  www.NPS.gov/getinvolved/volunteer.htm

"The excitement of learning separates youth from old age. As long as you're learning, you're not old."
—*Rosalyn S. Yalow*

"I am learning all the time. The tombstone will be my diploma."
—*Eartha Kitt*

For an Exciting Retirement

Perhaps it's time to think about going back to school yourself. Tens of thousands of retirees are attending classes. A large majority of those are attending school part-time.

Today's trend is to sign up for classes that will make life and retirement more exciting and perhaps more profitable.

Of course, you don't have to go to college for a continuing education. Your purposes might be served if you take adult education courses available through your public school system or one of the various organizations—perhaps your local Y—that sponsors courses.

CHECK OUT YOUR...

Local Library • Nearest College
Community Center • Local Y
Board of Education

If you have a lively mind and an interest in improving it, you almost certainly can find educational opportunities (often free or at a minimum charge) that can open up a world of vast horizons in your later years.

The sharpness of a mind generally is blunted, not by age but by disuse. This can happen at any age.

Those reasonably healthy can maintain skills and abilities well into, and perhaps beyond, their 80s. The ability to learn new things is also maintained. If mental responses are slowed a little, this is more than offset by the fact that the older you are, the greater your advantage in being able to apply your background of knowledge and experience.

So, don't hold back. And don't feel that it's eccentric to go back to school or shy away from being taught by a younger person.

Many are interested in making up for years when going to school was not possible. Continuing education courses offer opportunities to take high school level equivalency courses, leading to diplomas. In some programs it is possible to obtain credit for life experiences— Your jobs and activities count toward a degree.

Explore the possibilities of the many courses available that are intended to enrich the lives of adults in your community or to prepare them for better or different jobs during their working years or in retirement.

There are many exciting cultural courses: great books classes, lifelong learning, history studies, courses in art or music appreciation, current issues, politics, philosophy and similar subjects.

Some are practical. These often include income management and investing, health, home and auto repairs, legal and tax matters, sewing, cooking and the like. Courses like these can be invaluable during your retirement years, when money is tight. The skills you learn not only can give you personal satisfaction but also can save you money—a real inflation fighter.

Courses of All Kinds

Other classes are hobby-oriented. Continuing education programs include courses in such things as art, photography, crafts and golf and other sports. Hobby-oriented courses offer chances to explore ways to spend your retirement leisure enjoyably.

Many are directed toward present or future jobs. Courses in bookkeeping, computer programming, office skills, real estate, medical technology, and the basics of starting your own business are available in most communities. Costs vary greatly, but usually there is a senior citizen discount.

If you are among those who didn't go to college or complete college work toward a degree, now is a good time to get started. Or if you are among those with keen interests in any field, it's a good time to satisfy them by looking through a college catalog and signing up for a course or two. The range of classes is wider than in adult education programs sponsored by public school systems or local organizations, and the subject matter is probably more advanced.

Many colleges and universities run extension courses, also known as continuing education programs, in centers around the college area. They may or may not be credit courses—that is, giving credits toward eventual college or university degrees. While the costs may be high, discounts are often given to those in their 60s or older. Some colleges may allow you to audit a class (receiving no credit) for a nominal fee or free.

To find out what is available and what the entrance requirements will be, you should contact the dean of admissions (or the dean of older students, a relatively new post at some institutions) at your local college or university. Some schools have the same requirements for older applicants as for younger ones, but many do not require a high school diploma for older applicants whose backgrounds suggest an aptitude for college-level work.

If you take courses for credit, you will have to meet the same requirements as younger students: attending classes, doing assigned work, turning in papers, and taking tests and examinations. You also will be graded, but don't let that make you nervous. Surveys show that older students do as well as those in other age groups.

Courses to Fit Your Schedule

Those really interested in college may find weekend college programs in their area. Classes are scheduled on Saturdays and Sundays, usually lasting two or three hours instead of one to cover a whole week's work in a day. It's hard work but a good way to get a diploma.

All the above applies also to community colleges, which may be more convenient than four-year schools to many who are interested in continuing education. There are other points in their favor: local two-year colleges may offer lower rates or be free for older applicants, and ordinarily *anyone* who is interested can sign up *without* questions about high school backgrounds.

REASONS TO RETURN TO SCHOOL

To be accepted by others.

To satisfy an inquiring mind.

To prepare for community service.

To learn just for the joy of learning.

To seek knowledge for its own sake.

To improve my ability to serve humankind.

To maintain or improve my social position.

To stop myself from losing brainpower.

To provide a contrast to my previous education.

To help me earn a degree, diploma or certificate.

To overcome the frustration of day-to-day living.

To carry out the recommendation of some authority.

To share a common interest with my spouse or friend.

To improve my ability to participate in community work.

To fulfill a need for personal associations and friendships.

To acquire knowledge to help with other educational courses.

To help me gain skills to help start a second career.

To have a few hours away from responsibilities.

To get a break in the routine of home or work.

To become acquainted with congenial people.

To supplement a narrow previous education.

To provide a contrast for the rest of my life.

To gain insight into my personal problems.

To gain insight into human relations.

To improve my social relationships.

To learn just for the sake of learning.

To become a more effective citizen.

To escape an unhappy relationship.

To participate in group activity.

To get relief from boredom.

To keep up with others.

To escape television.

You may have heard about correspondence courses, either as part of college extension programs or offered privately. These can be a good idea for independent learning, though being in a class where questions are asked and comments are made is beneficial to the learning process and your enjoyment.

Be particularly careful when you see private organizations offer courses in computer programming, art, writing and other subjects—often with promises of "sure" employment or income. Check with a Better Business Bureau before you sign up.

You do not have to go to school to get a degree. You can also enrich your mind by partaking in programs offered at libraries, museums, galleries and educational societies.

One site to check is Seniornet, www.seniornet. org, which provides articles, chat groups and classes for seniors interested in learning more about computers.

TV offers much more than entertainment programs. In many areas, courses in general education or university studies are worthwhile whether you sign up to receive course material and to have your work monitored or whether you just audit the programs aired.

Now that you know more about what you can find in education, nothing should stop you from having a happier, more interesting retirement.

All it takes is a little time, a little energy, and some motivation to get you started on the way to being a younger-feeling, more alive, and more stimulated person.

see, retiring before or after the right time may lead to problems. The right choice will help to ensure a successful retirement. In planning, you should be prepared for the unforeseen. According to an EBRI survey, 50% of workers who planned to work longer had to retire unexpectedly due to a hardship such as a health problem or disability, and only 14% of people stopped working at the age they predicted.

Your Options

The Federal Age Discrimination in Employment Act bars mandatory retirement except under a few specific circumstances. Now, older workers must be assessed for continued employment solely on a basis of ability—not age. This means you have three options:

- You can retire voluntarily at your full retirement age (FRA) (see page 28) and begin collecting Social Security.

- You can continue working.

- You can take early retirement. The change in pension plan rules has made it easier to retire early but, due to the economy, 60% of workers are postponing their retirement. Those who are not covered by a pension plan may need to continue to work as long as possible.

> "The question isn't at what age I want to retire. It's at what income."
> —George Foreman

Retirement: Early or Later?

When should you retire? This is fast becoming the number one question on the minds of many workers. More flexible pension plans now give many workers exciting new retirement options.

American workers have a broader choice to make when they try to pinpoint a retirement age. For many workers today, the time span is from 50 to 70—a 20-year time period. With greater freedom in selecting a date for retirement, it is important that you choose carefully. As we shall

YOUR RETIREMENT FINANCES

	Example	Your Numbers
Income from last year at work	$40,000	_____
Experts estimate 80–115% of income to maintain your living standard	$32,000	_____
Estimated first year Social Security income (at full retirement age)	$14,688	_____
Income needed from pension, investments and full or part-time work	$17,312	_____

The above is for your first year of retirement. Ten years from now, with a 4% inflation rate, instead of $32,000, you'll need approximately $47,400. Social Security is indexed for inflation and, assuming it's not changed, will return approximately $21,742. You'll then need another $25,658 from your pension, work and investments to maintain your present living standard.

Current Social Security law gradually increases the full retirement age (FRA) from 65 to 67 by the year 2027. (See page 28 for a discussion of how your Social Security benefits will be affected by a decision to retire early.)

When to Retire

Whether or not you elect to stay on the job past retirement age, the option you choose should depend on your personal circumstances. You may want to quit earlier, take your pension and find an easier job. You may want to work past 66 or 67 to meet continuing high costs for medical care, children's college costs or other needs. Or you may be ready to quit at 66 or 67 to take life easier.

If you are a two-career couple, you should consider if you should retire at the same time or at different times. Separate retirement dates can offer advantages, including extending employer health insurance to cover the retired spouse.

Whatever you do, whenever you retire, remember that you face psychological changes. Idleness may give you a feeling of guilt and shame, a loss of self-esteem and withdrawal from society.

It doesn't have to be that way. In retirement, you must face yourself afresh. Keep free of self-pity and bitterness. Accept your situation, compensate for whatever losses might come, and remind yourself that what is important is not *what you've lost but what you still have and still can do*.

In short, learn to focus on retirement as a positive experience. Retirement is a new beginning; it gives you the chance to develop and expand your interests in ways that were not possible during your working years. Before retirement, much of your time is taken up by the day-to-day necessity of work. In retirement, the end of that routine means the beginning of new opportunities.

Early Retirement

Today, nearly 4 in 10 workers say they want to retire before age 65, according to the Employee Benefit Research Institute. In considering your options, remember that if you stay even a few extra years, you can dramatically improve your retirement assets, particularly if your job has a retirement plan and health insurance.

The reason today's retirees may stay working longer is primarily economics. They won't be as ready to retire at 55, or maybe even at 66 or 67, because of inadequate savings, reduced employer benefits and the possible scaling back of what the federal government will provide.

As the rules governing Social Security payments gradually change, with full benefits eventually not kicking in until age 67, that could be a further incentive to keep people working. Even without such a change in the rules, though, many retiring workers could be in for a shock at the size of their monthly benefit payments.

It is probably true that today's mature workers are better able to keep plugging away at a job. These 60-year-olds are healthier than those a generation ago. Moreover, fewer jobs now require heavy physical labor. Reeducating and retraining older workers could prolong their work lives.

To those asking the question, "Should I retire early?," you should consider these questions: Why? Retire early to what? Do you have a new life waiting for you?

For some workers, early retirement is not necessarily a free and happy choice. Many people retire before 65 due to the loss of a job, poor health or family members in poor health. A somewhat higher percentage of women retiring early cite such reasons.

If the work is getting too demanding, and particularly if doctors recommend taking things easier in your 50s or early 60s, retiring may be the right thing to do.

However, most people are still physically fit and able to continue on the job beyond their full retirement age (FRA).

Carefully consider the pros and cons of early retirement, the possible rewards and the potential pitfalls. Those who have worked for three or four decades may find inactivity difficult. They must substitute something for work.

They should have a carefully thought-out new life ahead. While that is true for everyone who retires, regardless of their age, it is particularly true for those retiring early. Younger retirees must look ahead not for an average decade or two, as those 66 or 67 must, but as long as three decades.

If you're going to start a new life early, ask yourself what it is going to be like. Early retirement is not for everyone. You must be ready for it and able to take it in full stride and enjoy it. Most of all, you must be able to afford it, not just at the time of early retirement but through the years to come.

Can You Afford to Retire?

You should be aware of the impact of inflation on those who retire. It is a problem that is likely to continue. While the rate of inflation has fortunately been considerably reduced, it is still a factor. A 4% annual rate of inflation amounts to over a 20% rise in the cost of living in just five years.

Remember, dollars are worth less year to year. It's hard to live with inflation while you're working. It will be even harder when you retire on a fixed income. Costs go up and, except for cost-of-living changes in Social Security benefits, the income of retirees may not keep up with living costs.

Retirement on a full pension and with full Social Security benefits is difficult in years of inflation. The problems will be considerably worse for those who elect to retire earlier with smaller pensions and Social Security payments. Assess how the changes in the economy will affect your pension, investments and retirement benefits.

Unless you can retire early and build up your reserves through a new job, a new business or a new career, you will probably be better off economically to work longer and concentrate on accumulating reserves for a more secure future.

However, dollars are not the only thing to think about.

Work satisfaction is another important factor in making decisions about whether to continue on the job as long as you can or to retire early.

Take into consideration that working a few more years can make the difference between a comfortable lifestyle or having difficulty paying bills. Even with the best-laid plans, circumstances can change your financial status. Plan for potential health problems, family issues and financial bumps in the road.

Retire to a Second Career

Do you have a job waiting for you? Remember, if you are considering early retirement, it's easy to talk casually about resting up for a while and then getting a new job.

But those who do not have highly marketable skills could run into a difficult time. Keep your skills current or develop new ones. Take a class.

If you are in your 50s and do not have a job waiting for you, be wary of retiring early unless you have sufficient reserves to make additional income unnecessary. You might find it's awfully hard to find the new job you now take for granted.

If you are considering early retirement without plans to take another job, full- or part-time, what then?

Are you really ready for all the leisure you'll have? Can you fill your time with community service, educational opportunities, hobbies, travel, sports, cards—whatever?

It sounds easy to do, but it isn't for many retirees.

Think about how many years you will have ahead if you retire early, and make sure, by advance planning, that you can make them active and fulfilling years.

Retire early if you can enjoy your later years free of financial worries and free of boredom.

Stay on the job if you aren't sure you can. (See Chapter 9.)

Making the Decision

Everyone approaching retirement must make the decision to retire at full retirement age (FRA) or later on a basis of individual circumstances.

RETIREMENT VS. VACATION

Many people plan their vacations with great detail, but not their retirement. Deciding to retire without planning can put a successful transition and a satisfying retirement at risk. Start your planning early.

The first, and perhaps biggest, question is: Do you need to continue working?

For example, are you paying off a mortgage? If so, do you need to continue receiving a regular paycheck to do it comfortably? Do you still have a child or children in college and need your regular wages or salary to meet steadily climbing costs?

Do you have some other important financial need that can best be met by continuing on your regular job beyond FRA? Under such circumstances, the ability to work can be a blessing.

If regular work is such a habit for you that the very thought of breaking it by retiring is a psychological problem, then perhaps working beyond FRA is your answer.

But remember, in the long run the substitution of new things—work and play and just plain relaxing—may be better for you.

Consider this: The longer you go on, the harder it will be to retire—and someday you will have to. It is easier to change a lifestyle at an active FRA than at 70.

You will adapt more easily to the things you would enjoy doing but haven't had an opportunity to do, and it will be easier to slip into a new, less arduous job if you want to supplement your retirement pay.

Before you decide, try doing the following: With the help of your employee benefits office at work or someone in the Social Security office, find out whether staying on the job beyond FRA would substantially increase your eventual retirement benefits.

For some, particularly those who have been jobless over long periods or have changed jobs frequently so that years of service for one employer haven't accumulated sufficiently, working beyond FRA could be a step toward a more adequate income in retirement.

Retirement Checklist

If you are considering early retirement, answer these questions:

■ Do you have something definite you want to do after early retirement? Is there something you have always wanted to do that you can undertake in your late 50s or early 60s? A second, deeply satisfying career, perhaps?

■ Is your pension plus your savings enough to bridge the gap between your early retirement and the time you'll start receiving Social Security payments?

■ Have you factored in inflation? If inflation were 4%, $1,000 of today's dollars will be worth $375 in 25 years.

■ Have you planned sufficiently for early retirement with your spouse and other members of your family? Planning for retirement should begin five to ten years before you retire.

■ Financially, are major obligations (mortgages, children's education, installment credit and the like) paid off or under control?

■ Have you thought about medical and hospital insurance between the time you leave your job

and group plans and when you will become eligible for Medicare?

- Have you planned for the unexpected: becoming widowed or divorced, developing health problems or taking care of ailing parents?

- Are you sure that early retirement will make you and your spouse—and your entire family—happier? That you really want it?

Check Benefits & Plan

If you're thinking about retiring early, check with your Social Security office to find out how much you'll forfeit in benefits and with your company personnel office to find out how your pension will be affected. Retiring at 62 could cost about 20% of the benefits you'd be due if you worked to FRA.

Before you retire, start checking on the documents you will need to claim Social Security benefits: Social Security cards; proofs of ages of both of you, preferably birth certificates; your marriage license. Get them together and in order.

Decide on pension options, medical insurance needs and options for handling mortgage or other financial obligations that will continue after retirement.

Decide, also, on whether automobiles and appliances should be replaced while your income is at maximum; it's generally a good idea to replace appliances over ten years old. And consider your basic clothing needs.

Above all, begin developing retirement interests and activities. If married, these should be both individual and joint.

Just Before You Retire

When your retirement time is approaching, here are some things you should do:

- Have a medical checkup while you are still covered by your company's medical program. It will save you money.

- Register with your Social Security office about three months *in advance* of your retirement. It takes that long to process applications.

Your spouse should go with you. Take the documents you need, including a copy of your last two W-2 tax forms, the withholding statement, and your spouse's tax papers if both of you are working. (See page 33.)

- Check with former employers to find out whether you might be due partial pensions based on their contributions to pension plans on your behalf when you were employed. Vesting plans vary. Many who retire lose money because they neglect to check with former employers. (See Chapter 2.)

- Retirement benefits are available under some conditions to war veterans with limited incomes or to widows of veterans. To qualify, veterans must be permanently or totally disabled due either to a service or nonservice injury. If you think you might qualify, check with your nearest Veterans Affairs office.

- Most important, make realistic plans for day-to-day living in retirement. You should have estimates of what your financial needs will be for living costs, housing, insurance, health care, transportation, utilities, clothing, recreation and miscellaneous costs. With retirement day approaching, review them carefully; in inflationary times, living cost

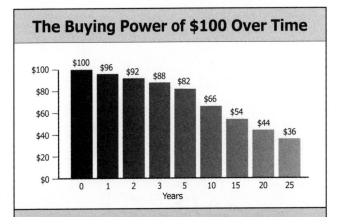

The Buying Power of $100 Over Time

The buying power of $100 decreases as the price of goods increases with inflation. This chart assumes a 4% annual average inflation rate. Social Security is indexed for inflation, but your pension may not be, so your investments should earn 4% after taxes to stay even.

estimates made earlier may no longer be accurate. In addition to estimates of what you'll need, reassess what you'll have.

- Sit down with a personnel officer of your company to work out exactly what your pension will be—and the options open to you in monthly benefits. If you elect to collect monthly checks payable only until you die, your income will be larger, but a surviving spouse will be left without pension checks. Your spouse will have to agree in writing to this arrangement. It's the law. An alternative is to take a lesser amount that will continue after the death of the retiree. There are a number of joint-life plans based on actuarial tables for life expectancy of the employee and his or her spouse. You should know your options.

- Check with your company on how and when pension checks will come to you, what options are open to you on accrued vacation or sick leave time (often you can get a lump-sum payment), whether life insurance carries over or must be switched from a group plan to an individual policy, and what could be done about continuing health and hospitalization insurance.

- If you are retiring but plan to continue to work in a second career, get a copy of the pamphlet "How Work Affects Your Benefits" from your Social Security office or at www.ssa.gov/pubs /EN-05-10069.pdf.

WHAT I MISS MOST IN RETIREMENT...

TO DO LIST!
•PAINT
•PLANT
•PLASTER ETC. ETC.

... ARE DAYS OFF AND VACATIONS!

In a nutshell, when you retire, be ready. Know what retirement will mean and how you will acclimate to it.

When You Retire

So you've retired. What then?

Your advance planning should have given you an answer to that question. However, here are things you should consider:

- If you have received a lump-sum payment from a qualified pension or profit-sharing plan, talk to someone at your bank or in a conservative brokerage or financial house about how it best can be used to meet your future needs. Don't consider the big check a windfall and go on a spending spree. Remember, it's taxable money. **You may avoid an immediate tax when you have higher income by having your employer transfer the money directly to an individual retirement account (IRA) within 60 days.** (See page 15.)

- If you enrolled in Social Security three months before retirement, your first check should arrive in the month after you retire. (See chart on page 33.)

- Depending upon restrictions in your pension plan, many retirees are able to continue full- or part-time employment. Check with your personnel or state employment office.

- Medicare provides hospital coverage after an annual deductible and a certain percentage of medical expenses after another deductible. Chapter 7 provides details of the provisions of both hospital and medical coverage by Medicare. These are subject to change by congressional action. There are supplemental insurance policies you may buy. Check their benefits carefully before you buy.

- Your tax position changes with retirement. Social Security benefits are taxable if your adjusted gross income plus nontaxable interest and half of your Social Security benefit is more than a base amount (the base for an individual is $25,000—for a couple filing jointly it is $32,000), but part or all of your pension will be subject to income taxes. So will income you may have from part-time or other work and from most other sources. Unless you take another regular job, you won't have money withheld to cover continuing taxes. Be prepared to handle more tax work—and tax payments—on your own. If you have any questions, call the Internal Revenue Service office for answers.

■ If you have your savings for retirement in growth and tax-deferred investments, check with your banker or broker about the advisability of changes to income and security accounts. (See Chapter 2.)

■ Consider ways to cut costs. Does your auto insurer offer a premium rate to drivers of retirement age who do *not* use cars to drive to work? Some do. If your car is more than four years old, check with your agent about dropping the collision insurance in your policy; it might not be worth the cost. And if you plan to buy a new car, check on insurance rates for the cars you're interested in: rates differ from model to model.

■ Reassess the adequacy of your home insurance every year. With inflation, repair and replacement costs are rising year to year. Be sure you are sufficiently protected against losses from fire or other hazards. Check with your life insurance agent as to whether you can convert your present coverage to a paid-up policy and save on further premiums. You may not need the policy.

■ If you want to work, there are agencies in most counties or cities that help older workers find part-time or full-time employment. Any local agency that works with older people can refer you to one. You may also register with an employment agency that furnishes temporary help if you have marketable job experience. (See Chapter 9.)

■ If you don't want a job but want to keep busy, investigate local volunteer service opportunities. Volunteers are in short supply everywhere. (See Chapter 11.)

■ Don't try to adapt yourself overnight to your new life and your changed circumstances. Go at it slowly and carefully, remembering that retirement is not an end but a beginning.

■ Check into recreation, education, community service—even politics—and civic activities that offer enough in the way of new opportunities to provide a sound basis for a new life in retirement.

Facts to Consider

The years you'll spend in retirement can be 15 to 30 years. Americans are living longer. Keep in mind that retiring earlier will decrease the amount you can safely withdraw.

Inflation will reduce the value of your retirement dollars.

Social Security is indexed for inflation. But the index doesn't fully cover the increased costs of medical care and goods and services.

Your pension may be indexed, but many are not.

Your investment should earn the rate of inflation plus taxes to stay even.

Health care costs continue to escalate. Medicare does not cover a number of health items that you'll have to pay for yourself. Check www.medicare.gov/what-medicare-covers.

"Age is no barrier. It's a limitation you put on your mind."

—*Jackie Joyner-Kersee*

Women Live Longer

Women live longer than men. That's a biological fact that should be kept in mind in retirement planning. Due to this, the average woman will have more retirement expenses than the average man. Most married women can expect a 5- to 14-year period of widowhood.

It's something we don't like to think about or sit down and talk about. Still, we must face the fact that an estimated 85% of all married women in the United States will be widowed. Regardless of age or marital status, understanding one's financial situation is of fundamental importance.

Women's Concerns

For many women, retirement is less financially secure than for men. Women on average earn less, live longer and are more likely to leave the workforce to care for children and parents. According to the Social Security Administration the average number of years worked is 44 for men and 32 for women. Divorce and widowhood also impact women's financial status. A widow can expect to see her income decrease by an average of 40-50%, yet expenses decrease by only 20%.

As a woman, your financial goal should be to replace at least 100% of your preretirement income. It is especially important to get actively involved in your financial future early. According to a recent study by MassMutual, women's retirement accounts were on average two-thirds the size of men's.

In a divorce, often one spouse wants to keep the house and may be willing to surrender other assets to get it. If you are keeping the home, you must determine if your post-split income will cover the mortgage, taxes and upkeep. For many, it's impossible to maintain the marital standard of living. You must consider if the assets you'd give up would be better for your long-term financial security.

One's Working—One's Not

Many people find themselves in retirement much earlier than anticipated. Meanwhile, their partners may continue to work. This creates a new dynamic in the home and in the relationship that can be difficult for both to adjust to. Together you should plan your retirement. Studies show that people often have different ideas on what to do in retirement, and couples who plan their retirement together are four times more satisfied with their retirement. So take the time to develop realistic expectations about what your retirement will be about.

	Life Expectancies				
Age	Male Expectancy	Years	Female Expectancy	Years
50	79.60	29.60	83.15	33.15
55	80.43	25.43	83.74	28.74
60	81.51	21.51	84.48	24.48
65	82.81	17.81	85.36	20.36
70	84.30	14.30	86.44	16.44
75	86.08	11.08	87.85	12.85
Social Security Actuarial Life Table				

The United States Centers for Disease Control and Prevention attributes the increase in life expectancy to new and better medicines, healthier lifestyles and lower reported mortality rates.

Many couples make the transition successfully. They approach their new circumstances as an opportunity—even if not welcomed—to start a new career or pursue long-put-off objectives. There is a need for planning, financial and otherwise.

Ask Yourself Questions

Women's longevity makes it necessary for them to face difficult questions:

- How many years can I expect to live with my spouse after retirement?
- How many years will I likely live alone?
- What is my life expectancy?

By now you've bought insurance, made your will and maybe discussed retirement with your spouse, friends and family. Have you, however, been realistic and honest?

With age, married or not, comes death of loved ones.

Along with the marriage partner, and family and friends, we develop a sense of interdependence. We share decisions and responsibilities, and our identity is strongly and inevitably intertwined. Our marriage and family life offer a source of love, security, emotional support and companionship.

The prospect of becoming widowed, of ending your shared experience with your spouse, is almost beyond thought. Still, you would be far better off by giving serious thought to how you can be somewhat prepared for that eventuality.

The purpose of this section is to provide a guide for that thinking. You can plan and prepare with your spouse as you always have and do it more securely and easily than if you were alone and under stress and emotional upheaval.

Being prepared is not an indication that you are preparing for the imminent death of your partner. The chances are that you have many happy years together ahead of you. But if an accidental death or fatal illness should occur, at least you will be in a position to carry on with and manage your life.

Widowhood: Being Prepared

"How can anyone be prepared for widowhood?"

It may not be possible to be ready for the shock of learning that your spouse is dying or has died. One thing you can do in this regard is to understand something of the emotions you are feeling and realize that it is good to grieve. Grief is the way our minds become reconciled to losing a loved one.

And we may feel other things besides grief. We may feel guilt—guilty for not having done certain things when our spouse was alive. We may feel angry—angry at being abandoned and left alone, at having to be without the awareness of where certain things are, or what needs to be done. We may feel lost—The old routines and patterns of living are gone. There is no one to eat breakfast with in the morning, and no one to talk to at night. We are at a loss about what to do or where to go. We may feel despair—despair so deep that we want to die. There will also be many painful days, including holidays, anniversaries and birthdays. We think back to what was and now is no longer, and we feel terribly down.

Afterward

The months following the death of someone we love are difficult and critical times in life. We have to deal with all kinds of emotions, without the help of someone with whom we used to share many of our worries and cares. They are critical times because we are starting out, on our own, to make a new life for ourselves. We will have to learn new skills, do things we never dreamed of doing, make friends and find new ways to spend our time.

No one can prevent this time in our life from being painful. People can help and will help, if we let them.

We may need the help of an attorney or a financial counselor for legal and monetary matters. There will be many matters to take care of involving taxes, property, inheritance, Social Security, insurance and the like. It will cost us some money to get help with such things, but it may cost us more not to. Very soon, after the funeral, we will want to take care of these matters: processing the will, freeing bank accounts, changing title on property, car, stock, etc., settling unpaid bills, keeping accurate and complete records, applying for Social Security and funeral benefits, and filing life insurance claims.

Other affairs that we must take care of, but that we need not be concerned with for a while, are income taxes, budgeting, seeing that our own will is as we want it, inheritance and estate taxes, and possibly others if there are minor children or dependents. Keep in close communication with a knowledgeable friend, or attorney, to be sure all necessary tasks are accomplished.

During the period after the death of our spouse, we may also need the emotional support that counseling, by a psychologist or minister, can give, particularly if we find that our grieving does not lessen after about six weeks. But most of all, we need to help ourselves. We need to find the power within ourselves to start a new life and to begin to discover who we are, what our potentials are, and what possibilities lie before us.

Decisions Widows Must Make

Many widows face, in addition to loneliness and grief, worries about budgeting and managing money, along with a lot of other problems that may have been a partner's responsibility.

For some, the necessity of tackling such new tasks is therapeutic. For others, it is added strain and more unhappiness.

One of the first and toughest decisions a widow must make is what to do with the money from insurance policies and from a partner's estate. She may suddenly have what seems to be a great deal of capital.

If she is inexperienced in handling capital, she could feel overwhelmed. It is a good idea for spouses to plan well in advance what can be done. Sound guidance is important—at any time.

In regard to family savings and investment programs, be wary, set clear objectives based on projected annual budget needs and get expert counseling, but avoid letting capital stay idle and unproductive because of uncertainties about what should be done and what should not.

Annuities can provide an assured income for life, but they limit flexibility. Once funds are committed, they **cannot** be retrieved or shifted.

Flexibility is necessary because of inflation, and needs vary. It's a good idea to explore the variety of investment possibilities early and establish a sound program that provides a basis for the use of insurance and other money by the widow.

Things to Do

Planning for both married and single life should begin in the mid-50s or earlier. Don't be discouraged if you are well past that point.

Assess your assets and debits as soon as possible. Summarize your whole family financial position. This is difficult if you left these business matters entirely to your partner.

For all women, *now* is the time to understand your financial status. Don't wait for retirement. If you set your mind to it and seek advice, you'll find it far less bewildering than you might have thought. It's just a matter of attention and faith in yourself.

Looking ahead to retirement: Even if it's a decade or more away, spouses should work together to prepare and maintain a careful inventory of what the family has. See Chapter 4 worksheets.

Too often, one partner assumes responsibility for handling bank accounts, bill payments, debts, investments and other money matters. They may be creating major problems for a spouse suddenly confronted with the need to cope with such matters.

The result could be headaches and heartaches for a spouse in a time of crisis—and possibly extra financial costs.

Women must have the knowledge of family affairs and experience in handling day-to-day financial matters if—in an emergency—they are to handle the chores alone. Shared handling of financial matters will make lone decisions easier. Working together, each of you will have a good idea of how the family stands financially. While this will not ease the grief, it can reduce confusion and unnecessary strain at a very trying time.

Will You Be Secure?

That's another question you have to think about together. Is one partner's life insurance adequate? If a spouse is retired, would his or her pension terminate upon death? If he or she is still working, would a pension program provide

REVIEW FINANCIAL MATTERS

- Do both you and your spouse review together your family's financial obligations and resources?
- Are both you and your spouse aware of where your money is kept (bank, investments, property, etc.) and the status of major policies such as insurance?
- Are complete financial records, including names of your lawyer, insurance agent, bank and broker, filed in an organized manner that a spouse or relative can refer to?
- Are children involved in money matters that affect them? Are they, or someone you trust, in a position to help manage your family's finances should the need arise?
- When divorced, widowed or remarried, now is the time to change the beneficiary on investment and retirement accounts, life insurance policies and annuities. Update health care, financial powers of attorney, wills and living trusts. If property was jointly held, update the ownership status.

for a widow if death occurs before retirement? What help would Social Security be, either way? How about health insurance? Married couples' retirement planning decisions should include the goal of leaving each partner in a financially sound position.

Know Your Pension, Insurance

Many workers do not know enough about their pension plans. They know, only vaguely, what they can expect in monthly payments after retirement. They have not read, or have forgotten, the fine print in pension material furnished by employers. Review all plans; in some instances a spouse can lose both pension payments and retirement benefits when a partner dies. Be prepared; a good way is for women to accrue their own retirement assets.

It is a good idea to take a close look at pension plans to find answers to the questions we asked. If you are getting divorced, talk with your lawyer about your spouse's pension plan; you may be entitled to a portion of your spouse's pension benefit. Be careful of trading other tangible property for your rights to the pension.

Check the listed beneficiary of IRAs, 401(k)s, stock investment plans, insurance and other savings plans that either spouse may have. Make sure you keep copies of your beneficiary forms in a safe place, along with your other estate documents.

You should check on what would happen to your widow's health and hospital insurance coverage, particularly under group insurance programs. If there are any provisions for extending coverage, explore the possibilities.

About life insurance: It's a good idea to review the amount of coverage you have in light of the rising cost of living. Coverage that might have

been adequate when policies were taken out might be inadequate now.

Social Security and Women

Social Security benefits will be continued for widows, surviving divorced spouses and disabled widows and widowers who remarry.

An eligible divorced spouse, age 62 or over, whose divorce has been in effect at least two years can become eligible for benefits, based on the earnings of a former spouse who is eligible for retirement, regardless of whether the former spouse has retired or applied for benefits. Widows with more than one prior spouse may have more than one choice of survivor benefits for Social Security. Check with Social Security on benefits you expect to receive. (See Chapter 3.)

Do Not Sign a Pension Waiver

Do not sign a pension waiver until you understand your choices. The 1984 Retirement Equity Act makes it easier for women to receive retirement benefits in defined benefit pension plans, either their spouse's or their own. A defined benefit pension plan is based on both your years of service and wages.

The act requires that in a *defined benefit plan,* a spouse must give written permission before an employee could choose a plan that would stop payments upon the employee's death instead of continuing payments to the surviving spouse.

The act requires the payment of a pension to the spouse of a worker who was fully vested in a defined benefit plan or had become eligible for the plan after working a certain number of years if the worker dies before reaching retirement age. The surviving spouse would receive the pension benefits at the earliest retirement age under the plan.

The act bars pension plans from counting a maternity or paternity leave as a break in service.

The act authorizes a court to award a person part of their former spouse's pension as part of a divorce settlement.

Important: The requirement of spousal consent does not apply in most instances to other savings, investments and retirement accounts such as IRAs, 401(k)s, insurance and stock participation plans. **Once again, it is very important to check.**

Survivor Benefits

Before retiring, you will be asked whether you want to receive your defined benefit pension in a joint and survivor annuity, a lifetime benefit or a single lump-sum payment. If the retiring spouse opts for the lifetime benefit or the single payment, both eliminate the widow/er's benefit. The retiree must have the spouse's consent and a signed spousal consent form.

The form will list options for you and your spouse to consider. The so-called lifetime benefit usually provides the highest monthly benefit, so people are tempted to select it. But it will pay only while the retired spouse is alive. It will end upon their death.

The joint and survivor annuity offers a smaller monthly payment. It guarantees a steady stream of income for two lifetimes, for the retiree and spouse. **For women who expect to depend on a spouse's pension as a source of income in retirement, the joint and survivor annuity is generally the better option.** For example, under a lifetime benefit while your spouse is alive, the pension might be $1,600 a month. While under a joint and survivor annuity, with a 50% survivor benefit option, the benefit might be $1,300 a month. But when your spouse dies, your survivor benefit would be $650 a month. Without the 50% option, you would receive zero.

Do not assume that your spouse understands the choices or the spousal consent form. Men also may not realize that statistically women are likely to outlive them.

The last chance to make sure you receive a survivor's pension is at the time of retirement. Don't sign away your rights unless you understand what you are giving up.

If your spouse worked for a federal, state or local government that does not require the payment of Social Security taxes, make sure he or she selects a joint and survivor annuity option for his or her pension, guaranteeing you a survivor's benefit. Unless you have your own Social Security and pension benefits, the spousal benefit is all you would be entitled to, with the possible exception of Supplemental Security Income (SSI).

WOMEN'S RESPONSIBILITIES NEVER END

Checklist
for Women in Retirement

Yes	No	
❑	❑	First and foremost, I do not sign anything I fail to understand. I refuse to be intimidated and will sign only when proper explanations have been given.
❑	❑	I will plan ahead, recognizing that (1) it is never too late and (2) it is never too early!
❑	❑	I am on top of financial matters: I know where important documents are kept—pension, insurance, Social Security, etc.—as well as the names and addresses of our family's attorney, banker, broker, etc.
❑	❑	My will is up to date, and I know where the original and copies are kept.
❑	❑	I have reviewed health/hospital insurance coverage.
❑	❑	If single, I have informed my attorney, banker, trusted friend or family member where my important documents are located, including my will and information to allow them to review my accounts.
❑	❑	I have a list of my spouse's passwords and PIN information to access e-mails and financial information.
❑	❑	I am taking steps to enable me to handle a budget and finances that may (or already have) become my sole responsibility.
❑	❑	I have looked into my own Social Security benefits.
❑	❑	I understand my pension benefits.
❑	❑	I pay attention to my diet—what and how much I eat and drink.
❑	❑	I engage in some form of exercise a minimum of one hour, four times a week.
❑	❑	I have a new interest: I've enrolled in a class, joined a group, etc. (See Chapter 11.)
❑	❑	I agree that "age is a triumph, not a burden" and that "in our old age we are free to be innovative, burst out and be creative."
❑	❑	I am prepared to face retirement with enthusiasm, faith and optimism.

"The delight I feel when any one of them wraps his or her arms around me, gives me a BIG hug, and says, 'Hi, grandpa!'… it's priceless."

—*A Los Angeles grandparent*

Did You Know…?

- In the United States alone, there are now at least 70 million grandparents.

- Nearly 5.5 million U.S. children live in extended families that include one or more grandparents in their household.

- Over 1 million grandparents raising their grandchildren are still in the workforce.

- More than half of grandparents help to pay for their grandchildren's education.

Close to one in four Americans are grandparents. There was also a time in your life when *you* were a grandchild, hoping for a moment of your grandparents' time.

So what does this mean for you today? Obviously, it will affect you most if you are now a grandparent, for this is one "job" from which you will never retire.

Grandparenting is both a joy and a responsibility, linking your working days with your retired ones. It provides a sense of continuity and stability

throughout the years, both for you and your grandchild. It is a way for you to keep feeling vital and important and to make a contribution that is meaningful for all concerned. It is "a relatively pure form of love and affection" providing you with companionship, pleasure and pride.

When the lives of parents are fragmented by conflicting work schedules and marital discord, aspects of the children's development may be overlooked. Should this occur, the love and guidance of grandparents can be so important. These efforts strengthen the moral fabric of the family.

To Be a Grandparent

"There is much grandparents can do to enrich their grandchildren's experience… Grandparents should be good listeners… communication is nine-tenths of a good relationship… They also play an important role in heightening the children's sense of security… They are symbols of longevity and the extent of the human lifespan."

—*Bill Bookman*, syndicated columnist

The Spice in Your Life

Studies have found that grandparents are second only to parents in the influence they have on children's lives. In doing so, you will also be adding to your own sense of purpose and self-worth. It feels good to be a good grandparent,

WORDS OF WISDOM

"Perhaps grandparents' most important function is as a reserve, to be there in case of need. Grandparents are the family National Guard, on standby duty to be called out in emergencies…. It's a positive thing that there are no strict rules on how a grandparent should behave. It gives them a lot of flexibility. They can serve a variety of functions precisely because it is so ambiguous."

—*Gunhild Hagestad,*
Northwestern University sociologist

- Contact your grandchild as often as possible. Visit if you live nearby or are able to travel. Make a phone call, send an e-mail, chat by video, or send a postcard if you live far away.

- Accept your grandchildren as they are. Don't try to mold them to your own vision of the perfect grandchild.

- Encourage and answer questions. Treat them as important people, and respect their thoughts and opinions.

- Be your grandchildren's playmate and friend. Set aside your crossword puzzle or book, and do what they want to do. Let them set the agenda.

- Take your grandchildren to the zoo, a museum, the ball game, or the movies. They'll remember the shared experience for a long time to come.

- Provide a link with the past; show your grandchild pictures of you as a child.

- Create memories and traditions. Tell your grandchild about your family history and traditions or your own childhood. Consider creating an oral or written history to hand down to your descendants.

- Show that getting older is a happy time of life.

- Share triumphs as well as misfortunes.

- Prepare a cookbook with family recipes.

- Give your grandchild undivided attention by reading to them. For older children, increase their interest in reading by sharing books for future discussions.

- If your grandchild has a yearly earned income of at least $1,000, you can give him or her that amount to invest in a Roth IRA.

just as it feels good to be a good worker, community leader or parent.

Your grandkids can add spice to your life, just as you can to theirs. And you can pass on family traditions and history to them in the process.

With the increase in single-parent and two-income families, you may even find yourself playing an important or stabilizing role in the upbringing of your children's children.

Grandparents can be a big help by watching their grandchildren during those couple of hours each day after they're back from school, before their parents have arrived home from work.

Staying in Touch

You can make a great difference in your grandchild's life just by making a simple phone call. Call up and speak to the grandchild, and when the grandchild says, "Do you want to speak to my mother?," say, "No, I just called to speak to you."

Increase your grandparenting power by joining your grandchildren in their world. Join them online. Keep in touch with your loved ones by e-mail, help your grandchild with homework, write a grandparent's newsletter and benefit by the many websites available on the Internet.

Long-Distance Grandparenting

You may be concerned that you live too far from your grandchildren to be an active grandparent. With modern communication and transportation, the miles can be easily bridged. After all, your efforts—as simple as sending a birthday card, calling to ask about your grandchild's schoolwork or activities, or telling the child a story about your own life—will form lasting memories for your grandchildren.

One of the most important things a grandparent can do for a grandchild is simply to be there.

Remember, a grandparent usually has a different role than that of a parent. Most grandchildren view their grandparents as a refuge from the daily demands of a disciplined home. Grandma and

Grandpa can give kids something their parents may not be able to give—enough time. This is one of the things they need most.

This type of positive grandparent-grandchild relationship can be fostered with just a little extra effort on your part, whether you are one or 1,000 miles away. A few minutes spent on the phone now will pay off handsomely later in the well-being of your grandchildren. And this, in turn, will make *you* feel better.

There is yet another possibility for grandparents who want to spend concentrated quality time with their grandchildren. You can invite your grandchild on a holiday or camp stay. Family reunions, combined with day vacation plans, offer retired grandparents a chance to select a suitable site and coordinate both transportation and various family schedules. These projects can yield rewards beyond what is required to make them happen. When traveling with your grandchild, be sure to take a notarized letter signed by both parents that states you have permission to travel with the child and to make medical decisions for the child.

Caring for Grandkids

Perhaps your concern is not that you don't see your grandchildren enough, but rather that you see them more than you had originally bargained for. With your grandchildren's parents both working, you may have the responsibility of supervising the children's activities during the workday. You might even be their primary caregiver. This is not an uncommon circumstance and can be trying at times. If you find yourself in such a situation, it can only help to look at the bright side.

You are not alone. An estimated 5.5 million children live with one or both of their grandparents in some capacity, and 1.1 million of these children are actually being raised by grandparents rather than parents. Whether this is a result of choice or obligation, you should know that there are plenty of others just like you, and that support networks exist to assist you with legal, financial and child-care concerns. Be sure to get legal custody; without this, you might not be

RESOURCES FOR GRANDPARENTS

For information on the Senior Companion Program, the Retired Senior Volunteer Program, and the Foster Grandparent Program, contact:

Senior Corps
Telephone: 800 942-2677
www.nationalservice.gov

Parenting.org offers tips, advice and information for parents, grandparents and caregivers of children of all ages.

Your local county or city Office on Aging, religious organizations, libraries and social services agencies will have additional information on resources in your community.

able to make medical decisions for them or gain access to their education or medical records.

If both natural parents of your grandchild are either deceased or disabled and your grandchild is dependent on you, the grandchild might qualify on your Social Security record. If the natural parents are not deceased or disabled, you might want to consider adopting the grandchild. When you do so, the child could qualify for Social Security benefits as your adopted child.

The value of your commitment to your grandchildren should not be underestimated. It may be hard work, but it's worth it. Your efforts will live on in the lives and minds of your grandchildren!

Remember, also, to take care of yourself. Your health and well-being are critical to the health and well-being of your grandchildren. While the opportunity to raise a grandchild may offer a second chance at parenting for some, the challenges and the unexpected demands of raising a grandchild may also result in stress-related illnesses such as high blood pressure and depression.

No Grandchildren of Your Own?

Even if you do have grandchildren of your own, you may want to lend a hand or an ear to other children in your community, as a surrogate grandparent.

Depending on the level of the commitment you want to make, you have several options:

- **Volunteer at a local school or hospital**, where your many years of experience will be your most valuable asset. Your work can be in almost any capacity—teaching, counseling, discussing or simply sharing ideas and thoughts with today's youth.

- If you are willing to make a more serious commitment, you might want to consider applying to the U.S. government's **Peace Corps** or **AmeriCorps VISTA** programs. With the Peace Corps, you can work with children, teaching anything from personal hygiene and the harvesting of crops to language and communication skills. Vista offers similar programs within the United States.

- For other opportunities, see the box Resources for Grandparents on page 115.

Family and Loans

Relatives who loan money should draw up a simple document describing the terms of the loan, including interest rate and schedule for repayment.

Before considering giving a loan, be sure that it will not destroy a relationship if it is not repaid. Be sure that you can afford not to be repaid and that the loan will not jeopardize your retirement. According to a recent *Money* survey, 43% of readers were not paid back in full, while 27% never received any payments.

In setting the interest rate, be aware of the IRS's applicable federal rate and that you must declare and pay tax on the interest earned. If the loan is over $10,000, you owe tax on at least a minimum rate, even if you don't collect. If you don't declare the interest, the loan could be considered a ploy to avoid gift or estate taxes.

Have a paper trail, both for IRS purposes and your own. Putting the agreement in writing emphasizes that this is a business arrangement. This will prevent misunderstandings. For gifting, see Chapter 4.

Guarantee a child's credit **only** if you are prepared for the risks. The Federal Trade Commission estimates that 3 out of 4 co-signers are asked to repay loans because the primary borrower has defaulted. Do not co-sign unless you can afford the payments yourself. Your credit score can be affected if your child does not pay.

Aging Parents

As you advance in years, not only will you have new grandchildren with whom to contend but also your own parents, who may be in increasing need of your help. This need may impact your retirement finances.

As a growing number of Americans become involved in caring for their aging parents, life care decisions and availability of support services become serious concerns. The challenges facing those caring for their aging parents on a day to day basis are many:

- Stress-related illnesses are common for the caretaker. Be aware of signs of depression. Seek professional advice, if needed.

- Delegate responsibilities if possible, and accept help from others. Suggest specific ways by which those who offer assistance can be effective.

- Learn more about your loved one's condition.

- Consider new technologies and therapies to help create independence.

- Ask other caregivers how they do it, and learn from their experience by sharing stories. Many receive strength in knowing that others have faced the same challenge.

- The Family and Medical Leave Act may entitle you to take up to 12 weeks of unpaid, job-protected leave in a 12-month period for a specified family and medical reason.

We are living longer, and so are our parents. With age can come difficult, sensitive problems of illness, memory loss and the need for constant care. This becomes particularly urgent when only one parent is alive or competent. Many of us live at a distance, sometimes thousands of miles, from our parents.

As we plan for ourselves and our children, so must we discuss and plan with our parents while they are active and healthy. Preparing now can give you and your parents the peace of mind that comes from knowing that you will be able to provide the help they may need.

Simple steps you take while your parents are healthy and active can ensure that no matter how far apart you live, you'll be prepared in an emergency. By taking action, you can prevent unnecessary costs and care for your parents in a way they would have wanted.

Respect Your Parents

There is no reason to treat your parent like a child just because he or she is growing older. Continue to involve them in your family by discussing all plans and decisions; make them a part of the process. Have them participate as much as possible in household chores. Encourage activities to keep them active, such as sports, hobbies, family events, clubs, organizations and religious participation. Try to develop routines, and stick to a schedule. Be patient and calm; if they have trouble hearing, speak clearly so they can understand you. If they are living alone, consider getting a help alert system.

Start Talking Now

You can help your parents stay independent as long as possible by starting now. It may not be easy to tackle the touchy subjects of aging and sickness by long-distance telephone. But whether you talk on the phone or in person, it's vital that you understand what your parents want and need and how you can help. Make a list of medications, Social Security numbers and contact information for doctors and health insurers.

Establish a communications network. Meet the people in your parents' lives—friends, neighbors, clergy, doctors, financial advisor— and exchange phone numbers. Make sure that you and your parents' most trusted friend have keys to the house.

Ease monthly bookkeeping. You can arrange to have utility and housing bills automatically debited from your parents' checking account, or sign up for programs that notify you if payments are missed.

Take inventory. Both you and your parents should know what assets exist. Learn where to find the paperwork on brokerage accounts, investments and pensions, as well as legal documents such as titles and wills. Talk about which assets can be tapped for assisted living or nursing home care, e.g., home equity or cash value life insurance.

Assess insurance coverage. Neither Medicare nor Medigap policies pay more than a fraction of the cost of assisted living facilities or expensive nursing home care; some long-term care policies pay for both, but buying coverage gets more expensive as your parents grow older. (See page 72.)

Check on Available Coverage

Your parents may become eligible for Medicaid but, to qualify, most assets must be depleted or transferred at least 5 years before people enter a nursing home. Each state has its own rules regarding income and asset limits. Call 877-267-2323 or visit www.medicaid.gov for a referral to the state office you need.

For a free booklet explaining how much Medicare will pay for doctors, hospitals and other providers, check www.medicare.gov/pubs /pdf-medicare-and-you.pdf.

Prepare Now for Tomorrow

Prepare for a crisis. Be sure your parents have a durable power of attorney, which gives someone they choose the authority to handle their financial affairs. (They may prefer a so-called springing durable power of attorney, which would take effect only if they become incapacitated.) Establish a durable power of attorney for health care or health care proxy; name someone to make medical decisions on their behalf; draft a living will, spelling out their wishes regarding life support. Download a state-specific health care proxy at www.caringinfo.org. Be certain, also, that they have a current will. See Chapter 4.

Home Care Concerns

It is estimated that as many as seven million people receive home health care through agencies or private arrangements. The reason is simple: More people are reaching old age, and almost nobody wants to go to a nursing home if there is a way to stay in their own home. It is also less expensive.

But there are problems. Federal and state rules that govern care in nursing homes don't apply in private homes. The industry is growing so fast and the demand for workers is so fierce that some less desirable individuals have entered the field. In most states, safeguarding regulations are inadequate.

Check all references. Ask doctors for referrals. Don't take the agency's word if you hire through an agency. And once you've hired someone, be wary.

Don't give any caregiver access to the patient's funds. Don't write blank checks. And keep a close eye on bank statements and credit cards. Consider having copies of bills mailed to a third party. As a rule, no caregiver, unless bonded, should deal with a patient's finances. Consider placing a freeze on their credit report on all 3 bureaus. See Chapter 5.

Be sure to have a procedure in place in case of an emergency. Keep a current list of telephone numbers and addresses of local ambulance services, hospitals, doctors and family contacts. Also keep a list of medications and medical conditions.

Finally, make sure care is monitored by a relative or friend. Signs of physical abuse, such as unexplained bumps or bruises, are obvious. Accidents happen, but repeated instances should raise concern. Psychological abuse is tougher to spot, but if a patient becomes withdrawn or starts changing established routines, a closer look may be in order. For more information, contact:

- National Association of Home Care and Hospice
  202-547-7424, www.nahc.org
- American Association for Homecare
  866-289-0492, www.aahomecare.org

Financial Elder Abuse

Elder abuse doesn't always mean physical harm. 37% of seniors have been victims of financial abuse. In its financial form, it's the exploitation of people to gain access to their property, investments, cash or real estate. The scams include identity theft, telemarketing cons, fraud by contractors and professional advisers, pressure to sign a will, or an empty promise to provide care in exchange for property. Sometimes relatives also commit such crimes. The abuser can be a caregiver, a family member, a financial professional or a stranger.

Don't leave mail in an unsecured mailbox. Shred documents. Have financial institutions send monthly statements to a trusted person to check. List and photograph jewelry and valuables. Keep items in a locked drawer and photographs in a separate place. Beware of telephone solicitations. Get caller ID. Block telemarketers; see Chapter 5. For additional resources:

- Contact your state's adult protective services

- The National Center on Elder Abuse (NCEA), www.ncea.acl.gov

- The National Consumers League's Fraud Center, www.fraud.org

Caring for Parents

Nearly 60% of adult children provide financial assistance to their parents. Many who become caregivers have no training and forget about taking care of themselves. Recent studies show that caregivers are more vulnerable to illness due to stress. Remember to ask for help and to give yourself a break. You must take care of yourself first. If you decide to become a caregiver, maintain your business and personal relationships.

For referrals to state and local eldercare information and service providers, contact:

- Eldercare Locator 800-677-1116, www.eldercare.acl.gov

- ElderCare Online www.ec-online.net

- Terra Nova Films www.videocaregiving.org

- National Institutes of Health www.nih.gov

- Family Caregiver Alliance 800-445-8106, www.caregiver.org

- Caring From a Distance www.cfad.org

- Aging Life Care Association www.aginglifecare.org 520-325-7925

- Administration for Community Living www.acl.gov

- Mayo Clinic—Healthy Lifestyle: Caregivers www.mayoclinic.org/healthy-lifestyle /caregivers/basics/aging-parents/hlv-20049441

The Eldercare Locator can also give you telephone numbers for adult day care and respite services, Medicare and Medigap information, tax assistance for the elderly and more.

The religious institution that your parents attend might be able to recommend a full- or part-time person who can help.

Assisted Living

More than 800,000 residents live in assisted living facilities. For those who are still in good health but need assistance with activities such as eating, bathing, dressing or medication management, assisted living may provide a feeling of independence and support. Evaluate your options; review the differences between home care, independent living, assisted living or a nursing home. Before choosing a facility, check out what services they provide: social activities, shuttle bus, sports such as golf or swimming, nursing care, access to medical assistance.

Review the terms of commitment; many allow you to sign up on a month-to-month basis. Check the social atmosphere, and meet with the fellow residents for shared interests in walking, card or board games, religious values, music, etc. If the facility provides meals, review the menus and be sure to taste a few meals. Check to see if your long-term care policy will cover some of the expenses. For more information, check:

- National Center for Assisted Living 202-842-4444, www.ahcancal.org/ncal

Choosing a Nursing Home

A nursing home is an emotional, medical and financial decision. Approximately one-half of all nursing home admissions come directly after hospital stays; the patient can have as little as one day to pick a nursing home. Planning will make an informed decision easier.

If a parent or spouse is unable to live alone, requires supervision, is chronically ill and needs help with daily activities and home care is not adequate, a nursing home may be needed. Before picking a nursing home, you must do your homework.

Ask for recommendations from friends and doctors. Involve your parent or spouse in the decision. Your state department of health or local office of aging can provide you with a list of nursing homes in your area. Visit the nursing homes with and without an appointment to review how the staff and residents react to each other. When you revisit the nursing home, go on a different day and time. Make multiple visits to them before you make your final decision. Talk with the residents, their families and the staff for their opinions and experiences. And taste the food. Review what services the home will provide: social, recreational, religious or cultural. Ask if they have choices with their living space, if there is a waiting list and if there is adequate security. Get the fee schedule for room, meals and other services in writing.

Nursing homes can be very expensive, and Medicare does not generally cover the care. Many insurance policies do not cover nursing homes; do not drop your health insurance policy, since it should cover hospital, doctor visits and some supplies while in the nursing home. Long-term care policies vary; be familiar with your policy. Read the nursing home agreement carefully before signing. If possible, the resident should sign the agreement. If this is not possible, you may sign the agreement, but only as the resident's agent. This way you will not be personally responsible for payments. Get assistance before spending a life's savings; ask your local area agency on aging, your state health insurance assistance program, your lawyer or your financial planner to recommend services. (See Chapter 7.)

To compare nursing homes, check: 800-MEDICARE or www.medicare.gov /nursinghomecompare/search.html

Planning a Funeral

It is never easy to plan for a funeral. Planning in advance makes the process easier. Shop around for the best price in advance; compare costs of the entire package, get a price list in writing, resist emotional overspending, put your preferences in writing and keep your plan in a safe place. Let a family member know where you file it. Specify which charity or fund you would prefer as the recipient of memorial gifts. A casket is often the most expensive item you'll buy.

Do not prepay your funeral expenses. Buying a small insurance policy or establishing a savings account to cover expenses will give you flexibility if you move, the firm goes out of business, or you want to cancel the contract. Consult the Funeral Consumers Alliance, 802-865-8300, www.funerals.org.

More than 2 million dead Americans become victims of identity theft each year. In an obituary, do not include birthday or maiden name. Mail the death certificate to all 3 credit bureaus to protect from identity theft. Cancel the deceased's credit card ASAP.

If you served in the military, you could be eligible for benefits. Contact the VA at 800-827-1000 or www.cem.va.gov.

Departments of Aging

National Care Planning Council state aging units administer and support a wide range of community-based services such as:

- Adult day care
- Group meals
- Legal assistance
- Senior center programs
- "Meals on Wheels"
- Visiting homemakers
- Chore services
- Friendly visiting
- Home health services
- Respite care for families

The Years Ahead

The National Institutes of Health (NIH) reports that most people are living longer and, when older, enjoying life much more.

Not too many years ago, there was an unfortunate concept that things ended abruptly at retirement age, 65 for most Americans, because one was old at that age. We now know that is nonsense.

The truth of the matter is that if you reach age 65, you will have anywhere from 16 to 19 or more years of life ahead of you. You can expect to live to about 81 as a male and at least to 84 as a female.

The longevity today has prompted the National Institutes of Health to note that there are three distinct ages after 65, roughly a decade apart and each with different characteristics. In looking ahead to retirement, or if retired and planning for later years, it is interesting to consider the NIH findings.

According to NIH:

The first age—from 65 to 75—is likely to show no substantial decline in capabilities. The NIH calls this period "young old," a continuation of midlife with only a slight drop in ability to take hikes, play golf or tennis or engage in other accustomed physical activities.

There are reams of data to demonstrate that when you are in your 60s or early 70s, your ability to recall, to remember, to reason, and to calculate numbers will be virtually identical.

Some changes begin to show up in the second age, from 75 to 85. Lives begin to slow down. We become less confident than we were before age 75.

After age 85, people concentrate more on making their lives comfortable and happy by relaxing more but remaining active by spending time with their friends, children and grandchildren.

In Conclusion

Retirement is a time of change, growth and adjustment. Sounds like a difficult time, doesn't it? Perhaps, but the best way to turn apprehension into confidence is by planning.

We hope that this book has helped you and that you are looking forward to retirement with anticipation, good humor and plans that are right for you.

AFTER SEVENTY

Pamper the body,
Prod the soul
Accept limitations,
But play a role
Withdraw from the front,
But stay in the fight
Avoid isolation,
Keep in sight
Beware of reminiscing,
Except to a child
To forgetting proper names,
Be reconciled
Refrain from loquacity,
Be crisp and concise
And regard self-pity
As a cardinal vice.

— *Oliver Higgins Prouty*

Benefits: The National Council on Aging (NCOA) has an online "Benefits CheckUp" program that finds programs for seniors that may pay for some of their prescription drugs, health care, utilities, and other essential items or services. Check online at www.benefitscheckup. org. Have your records about your income, assets and current expenses available.

Debt Problems: The nonprofit GreenPath, Inc., with over 600 offices nationwide, offers free or low-cost budget planning and assistance in working out financial difficulties. Check local yellow pages, call toll-free 800-550-1961, write to GreenPath Debt Solutions, 36500 Corporate Drive, Farmington Hills, MI 48331 or visit www.greenpath.com.

Financial Planners: If you need a financial planner (see page 20), you can find one through industry associations. The Financial Planning Association offers fee-only planners who have at least two years' experience and at least one professional designation. Call 800-322-4237 or visit www.plannersearch.org. The National Association of Personal Financial Advisors can be reached at 847-483-5400 or www.napfa.org. The CFP Certified Financial Planner can be reached at 800-487-1497 or www.cfp.net.

Make sure the advisor is registered with your state securities department and does not have any complaints (www.nasaa.org). Be wary of free retirement planning seminars.

Government Publications: For a free listing of publications for sale, call 866-512-1800, write Superintendent of Documents, U.S. Government Publishing Office, P.O. Box 979050, St. Louis, MO 63197-9000 or order online from www.bookstore.gpo.gov.

Estate Planning: For answers about trusts, living wills, power of attorney and other information, check the American Bar Association, www.americanbar.org/groups /real_property_trust_estate/resources/estate _planning/estate_planning_faq.

Health Care Resource: The Federal Trade Commission offers healthy living resources at www.consumer.ftc.gov/topics /healthy-living.

Insurance: For a brochure providing consumer information on life insurance, write to the American Council of Life Insurers, Company Services, 101 Constitution Ave., NW, Suite 700, Washington, DC 20001, 202-624-2000, www.acli.com.

The Insurance Information Institute, a consortium of life, health, property and casualty insurers, has a toll-free insurance help line. You can reach it at 212-346-5500 or www.iii.org.

Create an insurance record by taking photos of your jewelry, artwork and valuables. Include receipts. If disaster strikes, this will help you speed up your claim. Keep copies in a safe place outside your home.

Pensions: If your employer can't furnish a copy of your pension plan's annual statement, you can get one from the U.S. Department of Labor. Call 866-444-3272. Please provide your employer's name, address and federal tax identification number (it should be on your W-2), the name of the pension plan, and the year of the statement you want.

Record Keeping: Experts recommend that you keep bank statements for at least 3 years and tax returns and related paperwork for at least 7 years.

Medical records related to chronic and major medical procedures should be kept indefinitely.

Veterans: The IRS offers information for veterans, including information on free return preparation, disability benefits and legal services. Visit www.irs.gov/individuals/information-for -veterans.

Unclaimed Funds: About $42 billion is held in state unclaimed fund accounts due to death, moving or closed accounts. Contact your state controller or treasurer or search online for "unclaimed property" and see if they have you listed. DO NOT pay a fee for this service; it is free on your state site.

Hotline Information

Diseases & Conditions

Alzheimer's & Related Disorders
800-272-3900 • www.alz.org

American Academy of Allergy/Asthma & Immunology
www.aaaai.org

American Cancer Society
800-227-2345 • www.cancer.org

American College of Cardiology
www.cardiosmart.org

American Council of the Blind
800-424-8666 • www.acb.org

American Diabetes Association
800-342-2383 • www.diabetes.org

American Heart Association
800-242-8721 • www.heart.org

American Kidney Fund
800-638-8299 • www.kidneyfund.org

American Lung Association
800-586-4872 • www.lung.org

American Optometric Association
800-365-2219 • www.aoa.org

American Parkinson's Disease Association
800-223-2732 • www.apdaparkinson.org

American Podiatric Medical Association
301-581-9200 • www.apma.org

American Speech-Language-Hearing Association
800-638-8255 • www.asha.org

American Stroke Association
888-478-7653 • www.strokeassociation.org

Arthritis Foundation
844-571-4357 • www.arthritis.org

Better Hearing Institute
202-975-0905 • www.betterhearing.org

Eye Care America (Over 65 Only)
877-887-6327 • www.eyecareamerica.org

Incontinence Problems
800-237-4666 • www.simonfoundation.org

Lung Line
800-222-LUNG • www.nationaljewish.org

Mayo Clinic • www.mayoclinic.org

Mental Health America
800-969-6642 • www.nmha.org

National Council on Alcoholism & Drug Dependence
800-622-2255 • www.ncadd.org

National Headache Foundation
888-643-5552 • www.headaches.org

National Osteoporosis Foundation
800-231-4222 • www.nof.org

Government Resources

Centers for Medicare & Medicaid Services
800-633-4227 • www.cms.gov

Consumer Product Safety Commission Hotline
800-638-2772 • www.cpsc.gov

Internal Revenue Service
800-829-1040 • www.irs.gov

Medicare Information
800-633-4327 • www.medicare.gov

Social Security Information
800-772-1213 • www.ssa.gov

Substance Abuse & Mental Health Services
877 726-4727 • www.samhsa.gov

Health Referral

The Eldercare Locator
800-677-1116 • www.eldercare.gov

Health in Aging Foundation
800-563-4916 • www.healthinaging.org

National Rehabilitation Information Center
800-346-2742 • www.naric.com

U.S. Department of Health & Human Services
877-696-6775 • www.hhs.gov

Miscellaneous

American Dental Association
800-621-8099 • www.ada.org

Library of Congress National Library Services for the Blind & Physically Handicapped
888-657-7323 • www.loc.gov/nls

Road Scholar
800-454-5768 • www.roadscholar.org

Volunteers of America
800-899-0089 • www.voa.org